RUNNING THROUGH THE SWINGING DOORS

To Deanna—
Best to you!

To James!

Best to you,

Jim

RUNNING THROUGH THE SWINGING DOORS

ADVENTURES AND SORDID TALES FROM
LIFE IN THE RESTAURANT BIZ

TONY DI LEMBO
FOREWORD BY SUZANNE SOMERS

RUNNING THROUGH THE SWINGING DOORS

Adventures and Sordid Tales from Life in the Restaurant Biz

Published by Tony Di Lembo
330 East Amado Road
Palm Springs, CA 92262
info@thetropicale.com
In association with:
James O. Fraioli
Culinary Book Creations, LLC
Bellevue, Washington 98004 USA

Cover Photography by Tucker & Hossler
Cover Design by Scott McGillivray
Book Design by theBookDesigners

ISBN: 978-0-578-89928-2
First Edition 2021

Printed and bound in China
10 9 8 7 6 5 4 3 2 1

Dad, my first teacher. It's all your doing.
Mom, everything good in me, comes from you.
Ranz, we run together. Forever.

CONTENTS

"Nothing lasts forever. So, live it up, drink it down, laugh it off, avoid the drama, take chances and never have regrets because you'll find at one point everything you did was exactly what was supposed to be."

MARILYN MONROE

FOREWORD

by Suzanne Somers

A great restaurant requires great vision.

Out of the ashes of an old body shop, a phoenix would one day rise and seemingly, effortlessly, Palm Springs was blessed with the wonder of Tropicale, the restaurant where Tony and I would meet. Upon arriving, I float into what feels like the most spectacular party. The front desk is always genuinely happy to see us, and then from nowhere, Tony "appears." As he walks us past the live musicians playing Sinatra-esque party music, and past the crowded bar where Ranz, his partner, is there to say hello and adds to the hip and festive atmosphere, I am seated at my favorite table with fanfare and then, magically, my favorite drink is in my hand. Never would one have walked into the mess of broken-down cars and old car parts and say to themselves, *Ah, wouldn't this site make a perfect restaurant?* Well, that is the brilliance of what he does.

Tony grew up with great food. His father was a restaurateur and his mother and grandmother never wasted a thing, having come from that era where excess was turned into jams and marmalades and canned things. So little Tony was *hooked* from early on, not realizing what that meant. Many restaurants later, plus a stint as private chef for Ms. Streisand, our paths fortuitously crossed.

As I sit at my favorite table with my friends, I look down as Tony slips my cherished, crispy, tempura-fried green beans in front of me and then aaah, bliss, delight, serenity, and the party continues. The evening is a "ten"—couldn't be better by my standards—great food, great service, happy people partying and working.

It all seems so effortless.

So, imagine my surprise when reading *Running Through the Swinging Doors* to find that the behind-the-scenes is akin to backstage in a high-stakes Broadway musical. When one sits in a theater audience, one never thinks about backstage frenzy as things get dropped, mistakes are made, tempers flare, and crew doesn't show, yet out front, we are calm, entertained, and pleasantly impressed with the apparent control of it all. Always behind such composure is a visionary that makes the experience memorable and healing. Tony is that visionary.

PREFACE

*"There is nothing to writing. All you do is sit
down at a typewriter and bleed."*

ERNEST HEMINGWAY

Everyone should write at least one book in their life-
time and it should be about themselves and should
tell the truth.

Remarkably, mine actually happened, and writing
down my story provided a great deal of eye-opening
self-discovery as I looked back over five decades of professional pandemonium. It made me think about why I
took certain paths, and how they delivered me to where
I am. Writing about oneself sets off a divine out-of-body
experience, like floating above a surgeon's table, gazing
down at your life and seeing it as though from someone

else's point of view. The process is therapeutic and puri-
fying and helps bring sense to it all. And it's a hell of a lot
cheaper than sitting through therapy.

Hence, I wrote this book.

I have spent almost ten thousand evenings of my
life working in restaurants, and I can honesty tell you
that few have passed without some episode worthy of
a mention in these pages. Granted, most were benign,
maybe a rowdy argument at the bar that ended in a
tossed drink, maybe a drunk bachelorette found curled
around a toilet on the floor of the lady's room, or maybe
that time a spirited old soul dressed as Santa—bells on
his sash, antlers on his little dog—walked around the
restaurant and passed out Christmas cookies to the tick-
led staff. But for decades, shit happened, and I always
would think to myself, "God, I should write this stuff
down—another story for the book."

I remember the moment I actually began the process, the second I held my nose and jumped in the lake,
when I sat in front of my computer, opened a new file,
and a window popped up. As I stared at the monitor,
all I saw was a blinking curser. For a half hour, I stared
at that blinking curser, wondering how I could tell the
story, trying to jar this seasoned brain of mine to recall
some of the more notable events from those ten thousand evenings, and then suddenly, out of my fingers
resting on the keyboard, burst my first sentence.

It is said that when Dante wrote *The Divine Comedy* that he wrote one word a day and took almost twelve years to finish his great work. I get it. There were days when my output was zip, nada, a waste of a couple of hours at my desk, and other days, I frantically typed like a news reporter trying to make deadline with a breaking story, information just flowing out of me. More than once, after hours of writing pages, I would reread what I wrote, select it all, and hit the delete key. The delete key became my best friend. It allowed me playtime, to splash in the water with my ideas, and I quickly learned that when the story became too contrived or started to get confusing, a quick flick of my ring finger to that liberating, little button instantly transported me back home, back to the blinking curser, ready to start again. Draft after draft ended up in digital heaven.

What opened my eyes most during this literary voyage of discovery was the revelation that the dining public really doesn't know much about what goes down in restaurants. Their exposure is having dinner, and that's it. But I can assure you this—those who really know the sordid truth are the warriors who work there, the rock stars, the misfits, and the sweating kitchen culinarians who, along with me, push through night after night trying to make strangers happy. Restaurant employees are not a typical lot. Human resource departments in larger corporations would short circuit from the relentless assault of restaurant employee flaking—late shift arrivals, no-call no-shows, drinking on the job, emotional breakdowns, and the occasional fight that they resolve in the parking lot. No one gets the ruthless madness of this business unless you work in it, unless you're a line cook who's been buried with a string of printer tickets to the floor, "in the shits," as we say, or a server who's stood at a table and stomached the whining of some self-righteous jerk incensed that his steak is cooked medium instead of medium-rare and how his evening has now been ruined.

As the project progressed, the first hour or two of my mornings were spent with my cup of coffee, my dog snoring at my feet, and my computer monitor. Like playing the piano, as I wrote every day, with practice, I seemed to get better and better. Writing forced me to scrutinize everything. It taught me awareness, to pay attention, to savor the moment, and after writing for a couple of hours, I would carry this mindset throughout my day. It allowed me to analyze a cross-section of my life's timeline, as though flipping through old photos, reliving an experience for a second time. Sometimes, the memories would leave me filled with joy, like the stories I remembered about traveling and discovering how people cook and eat, and other times, I'd walk away from my monitor quite pissed off, having relived feisty customer confrontations or reading through the nasty responses some people had posted on Yelp. That whole Yelp chapter almost fell victim to the delete button because it didn't make me feel good, but the truth often does not. My testosterone-fueled rants to those entitled crybabies were my only way of telling them they were not allowed to behave that way in the world. It was time to grow up. What they would write and post online so greatly wounded the spirit of my restaurant-coworker brothers and sisters who read them, and me, so that the chapter had to remain—it is an important part of the story. It's part of the truth.

The process of writing about yourself, turning the pages of your mental photo album, pondering the events you lived and the people who spent time in your lane, is a revelation like no other. I remembered stuff that was long-forgotten, most of which never made it to the book because it seemed interesting only to me, but as a whole, it was certainly part of my catharsis. I didn't write too much about the emotional struggles along the way, like the stress this business can put on a relationship, or the sacrifices one endures from working every night, through all the holidays and birthdays, or the loneliness that comes from living in a foreign country for a long time—though it was all brought back from the past in my great self-discovery.

Day after day, as my manuscript grew, and as I got further down the wormhole, I began to accept the fact that one day, someday, I would have to share my literary journey with other people and let a stranger in. Someone else had to read it, and I had to begin putting myself through the massive scrutiny that was to come, subjecting my work to criticism and to all the literary professionals who were to politely say no. So, I picked a few people who loved me and respected me and whom I knew would give me the time to read it and the gift of an honest critique. For the record, I hate criticism, and I always react: "Well, they really don't know what they're talking about—they are just negative and judgmental." Then I pause and exhale and think, "Oh shit, maybe they have a point," and a bit later, I'm saying, "Thank you, thank you, thank you."

Editing becomes an addiction. It's a never-ending ordeal that sucks you in like a party drug—the more you do it, the more you *have* to do it. Every free ten minutes of my day was spent rereading, retyping, copying, pasting, and rethinking until my brain was mushy and my eyes hurt. I was obsessed, fearful that something was wrong or didn't sound right, and I'd be thrilled when I realized I found a better word. This process actually took longer than writing the book and continued until the very morning I clicked the send button to submit the final manuscript. The time had come to cut the cord. Interestingly, and all authors can attest to this, at the end of the project, when there's no more writing, no more editing, no more thought and decision, a great feeling of emptiness comes over you, like a caretaker who, after a year, loses a patient. Now what do you do? You find yourself missing your baby and it takes a while to accept not having it around anymore.

Over my ten thousand evenings, I've likely had five thousand people work for me. As you will read, they came in all shapes and sizes and it's to them that I sub-dedicate this book. Every single one made the conscious decision to give this lifestyle a shot—some for just a taste, others for many years—and whether it was bearing the brunt of kitchen chaos or having to smile at a table and tolerate a sometimes-insolent public, I stand and applaud them all with pride and gratitude.

More than anything, I wanted to write a book that I would be thrilled to find on the shelf that tells this story. Certainly, when I was just starting in this business, a snapshot such as this would have been marvelously foretelling of the world I was entering and may have made my journey a bit less rocky. But nonetheless, I kept my pace running through those swinging doors, night after night, year after year, with an aching back and sore feet and a hell of a lot of satisfaction. Arising from a business that's supposed to cook people dinner, this is my story. You know, from the days when man first scratched charcoal on the walls of a cave to present day, with our monitors and blinking cursors, sharing our story is truly a wonderful gift we have to offer each other.

SCAM

*"Someday, everything will make perfect sense.
So, for now, smile through the tears, and remind yourself
that everything happens for a reason."*

JOHN MAYER

Life humbled me as I aged. As the years passed, I began to realize how much time I had wasted. The further I ran the marathon, the more I set sight on the finish line—there was just something about turning sixty that dangled the prospect of retirement in my face. For company people, at some point, they might give notice, have a retirement party, and pack up their desks. But when you own a restaurant, how do you stop? I have worked many years to build my brand,

and I am integral. The food I serve and the relation-
ships I have nurtured have defined my life—they are
extensions of my persona. When I own a restaurant, it
becomes me. If I were to pull out, it would not be the
same. It would lose its value, worth only the price of the
fixtures. Guests come to visit *me*—it is my character that
has made it successful. So, why the hell would anyone
want to buy my restaurant?

*Dad used to tell me because everyone has their own
dream.*

Ironically, just about every business I ever sold was
not actually listed for sale. An inkling to sell was always
quietly resting in a dark corner of my mind, though.
Interested in buying? Ask me. That is precisely what
always seemed to happen. Someone would walk in from
the street and the negotiations would begin. Sometimes
it was a local family or a small corporation, once a big
company from Japan, another time a business partner's
golf buddy, and one time—well, what happened made
the front page of the *Los Angeles Times*.

I am six years deep into my most successful restaurant in
Los Angeles. The place is always busy, and the crowd is
muddled with celebrities and bigwigs among the faceless horde of the big city. Then 9/11 hits, the Towers
come down, and the business ends overnight. People

just stop going to restaurants. There are a few nights I actually don't do even one person, zero, as people stay home, scared, shocked, and outraged. In a business that relies on cashflow, it does not take long to run out of money, and I nearly lose everything. I reinvest my savings into the restaurant to stay afloat, and with time, it all trickles back. The crowds return and my head is above water again.

One Saturday evening, I notice a group of men at the front host stand. They catch my attention because they are all very tall, handsome men, impeccably dressed in three-piece suits—something uncommon in L.A., especially on a Saturday night. They have dinner and leave, and I think no more of it. The next evening, they return—four of them plus two more. This time, as they wait for a table, they wander around the dining room, scoping out the operation like pit bosses in a Vegas casino. Again, they eat and leave. Two nights later, they're back, still in suits.

After dinner that night, the server comes up to me and says, "The guys at table 8 want to see you."

"Why?"

"I don't know," he tells me.

As I walk to the table, they all stare at me. When I get there, the man on the end of the booth, as handsome as a model, stands up, reaches out his hand, and in a peculiar, unfamiliar accent says, "Hello, my name is Mister Edward. We are interested in purchasing your restaurant."

I grin and chuckle back, "Well, it's not really for sale."

With raised eyebrows and a big, wide smile, he says, "Yes, I know, but we want it."

I think to myself, *If you got a lot of money, it's yours,* but I say, "Here's my card—give me a call."

The next morning, I have a message from Mr. Edward inviting me to his office for a meeting. I phone my friend Howie, a very successful Los Angeles commercial realtor I had worked with many times before, and we decide to go together. When we get there, the office resembles one you would expect at a high-end law firm: two receptionists with earpieces and phones ringing, beautiful wooden desks, people running around everywhere, and most of them fit the mold of tall, handsome men in suits. As Howie and I enter the conference room, there stands Mr. Edward and five of his staff. We sit and he begins his story.

Mr. Edward and his team had recently arrived from Haiti. His company procures and operates successful restaurants. They have extensive capital, place managerial and kitchen staff in each, have accountants who centrally manage the businesses, and plan to continue to run the operations without interruption.

Howie and I just sit there.

He continues to explain that they already purchased two other local restaurants and mine would be their third. At one point, I stop him and say, "Just how much are you prepared to pay for the business?" He tells me his offer, finishes up, and we leave.

When Howie and I get into the elevator on the way out, I look at him and say, "I can't believe how much he's fucking giving me."

Within a couple days, Howie finds out the names of the other restaurants Mr. Edward was purchasing. They are reputable businesses not far from mine and they are, sure enough, in escrow. Howie also verifies that Mr. Edward's organization indeed has the funds to do this. I spend two sleepless nights thinking about what to do—I always knew how difficult it was to sell a restaurant, and here I had someone who wanted it for a lot of money and would continue the business. My employees would all retain their jobs, and I would have money to perhaps start something new somewhere else. It had been a rough year, and I needed a break.

The next day, I phone Howie and tell him to accept the offer—we have a deal. A week later, Howie presents me with a legal purchase agreement that has been signed by Mr. Edward, which included a $25,000 deposit into escrow. I am selling my restaurant.

The escrow process for selling restaurants is quite complicated. It involves releases from the sales tax board, vendors, other various agencies, and a large, formal, thirty-day yellow poster from the alcohol beverage control people notifying the public of your intent to sell. It must be posted smack on the front window of your business, and when this happens, it clearly announces to the world that you are selling. As the thirty-day posting date approaches, I know I have to talk with my employees. Plus, everyone has been asking me what these guys in suits are doing all over the place.

I have the dreaded meeting with my staff, which is an awful experience, like having to tell your partner you met someone else. Everyone sits there quietly and just looks at me as I explain that part of the deal is that I will still be around for a few months afterward to help with the transfer and that they would retain their jobs, but nevertheless, within days, I start to hear rumors that certain servers, cooks, and even my lead chef were planning to leave.

Now things start to change.

Sadly, as I observe Mr. Edward's team scuttle around my restaurant, it becomes quite clear to me that they have no idea what they're doing. They arrive late to open the restaurant, or sometimes, they don't even show up, and they have no concept of how to do payroll, or schedule, or even take reservations or talk with customers. They are horrible with managing employees, they reprimand servers in front of guests, and they just seem to blunder about and ask dumb questions.

You learn a lot about someone from the questions they ask.

At one point, Mr. Edward tries to convince me to have my daily credit card deposits transferred directly into his account and he says that each week he would subsequently reimburse me the total. He says he wants his staff to get accustomed to the accounting work. Well, I'm not that dumb. I decline his absurd request. Not until escrow legally closes, I tell him.

By now, all I can think about is being released from liability. The thirty-day change of ownership posting has now been satisfied, and every day the escrow company asks for more signatures from both me and Mr. Edward. By now, a few servers and a few cooks have given notice, my lead chef has decided to relocate, and I'm back to running the kitchen. I tell Mr. Edward he's going to need a chef and he tells me fine—he'll find someone. I have one more week and I dream about being free. What took me six years to build is crumbling before my eyes.

The day before the hefty purchase price is to be transferred into escrow, I receive a phone call from Mr. Edward. He explains that after studying the financials of the business, he has determined he overestimated the value and he wants a reduction of the purchase price—*a reduction of more than half.*

I call Howie, who proceeds to go absolutely crazy. He screams that it's bullshit and that we have a legally binding agreement that cannot be changed. "We can sue the motherfucker. Don't worry, I'll call him."

The next day, escrow is scheduled to close. Just before 5:00 p.m., I call Howie, who tells me he had left several messages with Mr. Edward but had still heard nothing. Howie calls me later that night and suggests we go to Mr. Edward's office the next morning.

When Howie and I get there, we walk into the elevator and go up. When the door opens, instead of seeing the impressive lobby and reception area, nothing's there.

I check to see if we're on the right floor. We are.

Phone lines and wires are lying all over the carpet. We walk to the back. It is empty—completely empty. Nothing there. No fancy wooden desks, no partitions, no phones, no fax, no stylish conference room, no papers, and no people. The entire office that had occupied most of the floor of the building is now vacant.

It's dead quiet.

I turn to Howie and say, "I'm fucked."

One week later, we still have no idea what happened.

What I do know is that I am still the owner of a restaurant that has now been ravaged. Every night, fewer people come, and I am losing servers and cooks and my is chef gone. I can barely pay invoices and, from an accounting standpoint, it is an overwhelming nightmare. Within two months, as Mr. Edward's people mismanaged things, my beautiful restaurant has fallen from the sky and crashed to the ground. I am more depressed than ever before in my life. I would often cry on the way home.

Another week passes and Howie shows up at my office one afternoon. He sits down, looks at me, and says, "You are not going to believe this."

The escrow company called Howie that morning. They were notified by the FBI that Mr. Edward had been under surveillance for racketeering and money laundering. His scheming was first detected in Miami and he had subsequently fled to Los Angeles. Two nights before our escrow was to close, Mr. Edward and his team packed up and relocated to Houston. There, he was picked up by the feds and arrested. He was now in jail, held without bond.

Holy shit.

The other two restaurants in Mr. Edward's scam had lost even more money since they actually allowed him to transfer the restaurants' daily credit card deposits to his account. Thank God I hadn't done that. One of the restaurants had already closed; the other would soon close. The FBI confiscated all escrow deposits that were held for all three businesses. At the end of this horrifying nightmare, all I have left is the shell of a dying six-year-old restaurant.

At this point, I tell Howie to just list it for sale. Four months later, it finally sells, but during that time, every day is an unbearable struggle. I am completely broke and have to pay vendors with cash just to get supplies. I can't pay rent, or my home mortgage, and am overcome with debt. It seems like every day someone is serving me papers. I manage to make one final payroll for the remaining staff with money I borrow on my last credit card. I'm very close to putting my dog in the car and just driving away.

This time, at the close of escrow, things go smoothly, though up until the very last hour, there are many issues like liquor and food inventory agreements, liability releases, back-owed rent, licensing matters, utility transfers, and handling the slew of delinquencies. Shortly before 5:00 p.m. one final afternoon, Howie calls me and says the wire transfer has gone through—it is done. I do not own the restaurant any longer. I had already shut the doors a few days earlier to give me and the few staff who stuck with me a chance to close things down. The new buyer has plans to remodel and open something completely different. It's time for their dream.

That evening, as I walk out for the last time, I stand alone in the dining room. It is quiet, still, and has no lifeforce. It has passed away, and though I am sad, I feel a welcome peace that there will be no more stress. I stood in the very same spot seven years earlier when bulldozers pushed dirt around to level the foundation. I can remember putting the place together: how the booths did not fit when they were delivered; how the patio fountain leaked so bad, it had to be rebuilt; and how exhilarating it was the first time the power was switched on after a year of construction—you could literally feel the surge of energy flow through the building. I remember how the plumbers walked off the job because they got into a fight with the concrete guys. I notice last week's schedule still posted on the wall and wonder what would become of the people who worked for me, some for many years, as they move on to other chapters in their lives. I think about what changes the new guy is going to make and what his menu will be like and if he will keep any of the original elements, like the floor-to-ceiling glass wall that separates the dining room from the show kitchen. After a minute or so, with a final sigh, I turn off the power at the breaker, and I leave.

I never made it back to the new place after it opened, though I heard the space had been completely gutted and redesigned. Guess I didn't really want to see it again.

You just have to keep walking forward in life.

ROOTS

*"What you think, you become. What you feel, you attract.
What you imagine, you create."*

BUDDHA

As far back as I can remember, I have been surrounded by people who shared my passion for cooking and eating wonderful foods. When I was a young boy, the first words I heard my mother speak every morning had to do with dinner that night. Dad was a restaurant owner, and when he wasn't working, he talked about the business. When evening came, my mother had prepared a meal from her heart, inspired by her profound love for cooking and giving the best to her family.

Almost everything Mom made was from scratch—crusty breads, fresh soups, home-preserved tomatoes for sauces and pizzas, homemade sausages and pastas, dill pickles, fruit preserves, cakes, and pies. Half of our backyard was a garden, and when autumn arrived, we picked bushels of tomatoes and canned them in Mason jars, which was a full day's project that involved relatives and neighbors, always guided by my mother. A cold room off the garage in our Pennsylvania home served as the pantry, and its wooden shelves were lined with jars of tomatoes, peppers, cherries, pickles, peaches, relishes—just about anything you could pack in a jar—and they were used until the next harvest. As my school friends talked about how much they liked SpaghettiOs and Chef Boyardee, my mother was preparing home-made pastas and sauces.

Around that time, I realized something very rare was going on in my family.

Mom's parents were farmers, and most often their meals came from the farm—fresh-picked vegetables or a catch of freshwater bass from a pond, filleted by my grandfather and handed to Grandma, who would quick-fry them with a clove of garlic and a sprig of thyme. My boyhood summers were spent on their farm, and the activities of the day always seemed to center around food. Breakfast would include homemade sausages and eggs that had been snatched from beneath the chickens in the coop. There were slices of just-picked tomatoes with olive oil and basil and warm, crusty bread. And there was always a jar of Grandma's renowned (at least in her neighborhood) crabapple jelly, an anticipated treat she made every fall when the branches from the ancient crabapple tree on the side of the house would hang to the ground, filled with tart, little crabapples. Later, we would pick blueberries in a field for an hour, then sit and watch her bake them into one of her luscious fruit pies.

During the holidays, she would make her celebrated *cappelletti* soup—small tortellini-like ravioli filled with minced roasted meats and Parmesan, sealed with a twist of her fingers, cooked in water, and served in a steaming bowl of broth made from an unfortunate old rooster (that was the best). She'd take days to literally make thousands of these *cappelletti*, and her special soup would always start off Christmas dinner. Just being in the kitchen watching, talking, laughing, and eating was always important, always special, in my mother's family.

And there I was in the middle of all this.

The other side of the family wasn't much different. My paternal grandfather made the wine. Each autumn, he set up the old wooden press he brought from Italy and everyone would gather for the event, vigilantly overseen by my dad and my grandfather. There was always food everywhere, like trays of Grandma's wonderful homemade sausage. Just before fall, she would season piles of ground pork, stuff it into hog casings, and twist them into links. She would then air-cure the long loops of links during the cold autumn months on wooden poles in the cellar. When it was hardened and cured, she would pack large glass jars with the sausages and top them off with olive oil. For the rest of the year, her sausage was at every gathering.

The best chefs had grandmas who were good cooks.

Christmas Eve was the feast of the seven fishes, of which my favorite was always *baccalá*, salt cod simmered and then flaked with olive oil, garlic, and a pinch of red chili. Christmas dinner was an event that took weeks to prepare. The pastas and ravioli were rolled and stuffed by hand. There was a particular sausage made from diced pigs' ears and snoots stewed with tomatoes, garlic, and oregano and served with finger-rolled potato *gnocchi*. It was a tradition as old as anyone could remember, and it came to me through Grandma from my great-great grandparents who farmed the Abruzzi mountains of Italy.

I can still see her stirring huge pots of bubbling *polenta* for an hour. She would then pour the steaming porridge onto a large, wooden board the size of her kitchen table, spreading it with her special tomato sauce and then tossing handfuls of Parmesan all over the top. The family would sit around the table with forks in hand and eat off the board, drinking the tannic red wine that my grandfather poured and poured. A dark-roasted coffee after the meal always accompanied Grandma's lemon and anise *pizzelle,* wafer-like cookies made by squeezing a soft dough between the griddles of a hand-cast waffle iron that she brought over from Italy, passed on to her from her mother. As a boy, I remember watching her stand at a small gas stove, holding the iron over a flame, cooking one cookie at a time, and timing each side by mumbling to herself a thirty-second Hail Mary prayer, since it was just the right amount of time for each one.

As I grew older, I realized my love affair with food went back to my infancy, to the days when my mother held me with one arm and kneaded bread with the other. Cooking made us all happy. It was how we showed our love for each other.

I always knew in my soul I had to be a chef.

Years later, after college, I took a job selling business office equipment, and after working in the real world for a couple years, it became quite apparent to me this wasn't what I was meant to do, and I decided to attend a professional culinary school I'd been hearing about. The Culinary Institute of America was reputed to be the best, and in a surprising move to everyone I knew, I quit my job and moved to New York to begin the two-year program. Most of the students were late teenagers, just out of high school, had never even lived away from home, and seemed more interested in partying and scoring bags of weed than learning. I was different. I had already spent four years lost in college studying mind-numbing subjects of little interest and had worked in the competitive business world. For me, attending a cooking school fed my passion. I *loved* going to class. I loved sitting in a room and having a chef explain how to bone a duck, or how to make Hollandaise sauce, or the science behind why whipped egg whites puff a soufflé.

School is quite a different experience when you pay your own way and go to learn, not to just earn a degree.

The instructors were mostly seasoned, old, retired chefs who had worked through the years and had survived the truth. They taught us how to properly handle food, basic cooking skills, food costing, inventory procedures, catering, wines and spirits, and on, and on. These days in my life, having lived through many decades of reality, it's now obvious to me that much of this was theory, but that's what most of formal education is. The practicality of costing an entrée as they suggested, measuring each ingredient's cost down to the salt and pepper and determining a sales price, for example, is absurd. No one has time for such futility, especially in a busy restaurant where you are inundated with daily crises. Some of these chefs were real characters, like the guy who taught the breakfast class, Chef Blanchet, a stocky, retired French man with a thick moustache and bulging eyes who'd walk around class with a cup of black coffee in his hand, screaming in the faces of students like an insane drill sergeant. His accent was so thick, you could barely understand him, and if you were one minute late to his 4:00 a.m. class, he'd humiliate you and send you away. As fearsome as we all were, we knew this guy was an old pro. One morning, after a *week* of his French screaming, we sat anxiously in class, waiting for him to walk in. As he stood in front of the class, Chef Blanchet said, in a heavy New York accent, "My real name is George. I was born in The Bronx and I ride a Harley. The French accent I've been using was to demonstrate to you how easily we judge people by who they say there are, how they act, and how they sound." From that moment on, he was his natural self: kind, funny, and a bit of a wise ass. Lesson learned.

When I graduated, I knew there was so much more to discover. I was in my twenties, physically fit, and hungry to learn. It was time to find out how other people lived and ate.

I heard that cook apprentices, known as *stages*, are common in high-end European restaurants and bakeries.

They work without pay for a brief time in another chef's kitchen to learn new cuisines and techniques and to understand what makes particular restaurants exceptional. This excited me, and twelve days after graduation, I sold my car, put the cash in my pocket, bought a one-way ticket across the ocean, and spent a life-changing two years working in restaurant kitchens in Italy and France, discovering the art in cooking. I soon realized how relatively little I knew and how much more there was to learn.

What was most astonishing during this great adventure was the enthusiasm I felt from everyone and how those I met enjoyed teaching and sharing what they knew—I never felt in the way or bothersome. On the contrary, cooks pulled me aside to show me something, to share a secret only a select few could know. They would grab a fish and demonstrate how to clip the fins, or how to drizzle a stream of boiling sugar into beating egg whites to make a perfect meringue. Once, I sat on a low stool in a musty room off the side of the kitchen with two old Italian ladies who spent a good part of every morning making tortellini. One by one, they twisted a small pinch of meat in a pasta square and, with a quick flick of their fingers, produced a perfect little bundle. It was such a joy for them to show this young American cook how it is done, giggling when I made a mistake, or grinning with pride when

I did it right. I sat with them for hours and listened to their stories. And they listened to mine.

The kitchens in all the remarkable restaurants I visited were not the large, shiny, stainless versions you find in America. Instead, they were small, country-style rooms with a stove, an oven, a grill, and a large, center table on which plates of food were put together. Food was delivered early in the morning, usually by local farmers, and the menus would change every couple of days, inspired by what they dropped off. One man would bring herbs and greens; another would bring poultry, another truffles, and another fish, often still flapping in water. There was a great comradery among everyone—the cooks, the chef, the owner, and the vendors, interacting as though they were a real family of brothers and sisters.

One of my most special memories comes from the first restaurant at which I worked, San Domenico, located in a small town hidden in the Italian countryside near Bologna. In one of those being-in-the-right-place-at-the-right-time moments, the owner offered me a job in the kitchen of his two Michelin-star restaurant. He was a man of impeccable style and had converted his childhood home to what many consider not only the finest restaurant in Italy, but one of the best in the world. It was truly remarkable. The dining room was filled with antiques, silver, and Austrian crystal, and the wine cellar was a lingering, candlelit tunnel burrowed underneath the restaurant that displayed the most comprehensive selection of European wines imaginable, both young and very, very old. But what made San Domenico the most renowned restaurant in Italy was, of course, its food.

Valentino, the chef, worked for years in the kitchens of Paul Bocuse, the high father of nouvelle cuisine, and would insist that all supplies for the day's service were brought to the restaurant promptly at 8:00 a.m. I reported to the kitchen early my first morning, as anxious as one could be, and awkwardly stood next to a bunch of international young cooks quietly sipping espresso. Suddenly, the back door of the kitchen flew open and in walked a local farmer with six live chickens hanging upside down in his fingers. Chef Valentino snappily picked me and two other poor chaps to dress these chickens for service—not something I normally did. Fortunately, I had lost most of my squeamishness years earlier while watching my grandfather perform the task on the farm and was guided by the two other cooks. Moments later, a crooked peasant farmer burst into the kitchen with a large burlap sack over his shoulder and unloaded onto the center table pounds and pounds of large, fresh white truffles. I could have bought a car with what they cost. The aroma permeated the restaurant for weeks, until we had finished scrubbing them clean and preserving them in jars for use throughout the year. The *stages* at San Domenico were from all over the world and we were all there for the same purpose—to learn from the best.

It was difficult to leave San Domenico, but I knew I had to push on. Valentino phoned a friend who owned a restaurant on the Liguria coast near Genoa, and off I went. Here, a robust Chef Angelo operated a restaurant simply called Angelo's, and he was considered by many to be one of the finest authorities on Italian cuisine. His knowledge of Italian food was extensive. His inspirations were earthy and always based on strict Italian tradition, reminiscent of my days with my grandmothers. The freshness of everything could be sensed. Vegetables were picked and received daily, and the fresh herbs he used were nurtured in the garden just outside his kitchen. Often, Chef Angelo would take the guests' pasta to their table still boiling in a pot of salt water and keep it there while he made a sauce tableside. He'd then strain the pasta into the sauce, flip it around a few times, then swirl a big forkful on their plate, throw on Parmesan, smile, and exclaim: *Buon Appetito!* It was theater at its best. He taught me more than anyone about basic flavor combinations, what works with what, and why. For the months I was with him, I never stopped learning.

I had been hearing of a restaurant in Milan since the first day I landed in Italy and had to see for myself what everyone was talking about. A small place, La Scaletta, had a two-month waiting list for dinner. Both locals and international celebrities kept the phone ringing in hopes of experiencing its joy. The kitchen walls were covered with autographed glossy prints of famous patrons as well as restaurant reviews and awards. The restaurant belonged to Signora Pina Bellini and her son, Aldo, who oversaw the dining room while his mother worked daily wonders in the kitchen.

Signora Pina served her apprenticeship in France many years earlier when, as she told me, "It was unheard of for a woman to work in a professional kitchen. They simply didn't allow it." Now, forty-five years later, she ran her own restaurant and performed for only fifty fortunate people every evening. There wasn't really a menu. She chatted with her guests for a while, then cooked for them. Her knowledge of cuisine, both classical and nouvelle, astonished me time and time again. Her repertoire seemed endless, and she was always willing to share anything she could with me. The kitchen featured a center island where cooks would all synchronize and plate a table's dinner at the same moment. Chef Pina conducted the orchestra and personally inspected each plate before the silent waiters carried them to the dining room. I would have liked to spend years at her side.

And so it went, staging in restaurant after restaurant. What intrigued me the most was that, for the first time,

I was surrounded by *professionals* whose greatest joy sincerely came from preparing an exquisite dish. The conversation at a meal was always about what was on the table, just as it had been when I was a boy. We talked about the balance of the herbs or what a perfect accompaniment to the dish something else might have been, or how a great wine would work, or how we could make something even better the next time, or what we were going to prepare tomorrow. It was love for cooking and love for eating.

Then, one day, it was time to go back home—time to move on from some of the best moments of my life. I took so much with me when I left and, hopefully, I left behind something, as well. When I returned to the states, what I had seen, and what I had eaten, had made a profound mark on me.

DIVA

"Divas are not made, they are born."

FIONA APPLE

The plan was New York, that great culinary metropolis, home of the finest restaurants in America, the ones that stirred risottos to order and shaved white truffles over everything. This is where I intended to build a career in food. As fate would have it, I happened to land an interview for a job as chef in a new restaurant, but it was being built in a mysterious place to me called Los Angeles. All I knew of the city was that it was home to celebrities, and it was swathed in sunshine. I was sent an airline ticket for the interview, and though thrilled to be potentially involved in this new venture, I declined the position since the project was still a year away from becoming a reality and I was ready to work. One evening before I flew home, I went to a small party with an old friend from culinary school who lived in L.A. Someone at the party had mentioned that his roommate knew a woman who worked for Barbra Streisand, and that they were looking for a full-time personal chef but were having a tough time finding the right person. I left my phone number with him to give to his roommate, but I had no real hopes anything would come of it.

The next day, the day before I was flying back, I received a call from Barbra's secretary inviting me to interview for the job. I couldn't believe it. I thought if I could just meet her, the fan that I was, I could forever tell the story of meeting this great woman.

When I arrived for the interview, I announced my name at her front gate and drove up the S-curved drive-way through the sprawling Beverly Hills estate where I was met by her secretary, who escorted me to their office. The secretary seemed frazzled and disheveled, as though she were having a day from hell—she was certainly not inviting or friendly. I was soon to realize this was her norm—working for her demanding boss seemed borderline abusive. She was always stressed and running to make sure everything was perfect from early in the morning to late at night. She looked like she needed a good sleep.

The office walls where I waited for Barbra were covered with framed accolades from her career—dozens of
platinum albums, photos of her with prime ministers,
presidents, the queen of England, and every celebrity you could think of. Long shelves displayed all the
shiny statues from all the awards. I immediately noticed
the phone lines did not stop ringing and were usually
answered by another lady in the back. Barbra's secretary started asking me questions but was repeatedly
distracted by phone calls and other people walking in
and out of the office. Her questions were strange to me,
such as, "Ah, what do you like to cook?" Then the phone
would ring again. At one point she said to me, "Barbra
just called. She's on her way here and she wants to meet
you. Let me take you to her office."

We walked to the main house and to Barbra's office
where I was left alone to sit and wait. It was hot and
stuffy and dead quiet. The room was decorated beautifully, plucked from the pages of a design magazine—
everything was pristine white, including a white baby
grand piano draped in white lace and an immense white
lacquered desk. As I sat there, I could feel my heart
anxiously pumping under my shirt. After almost a half
hour, I was starting to doze off in the airless room. As
my eyes were closing, suddenly the door opened and
there she was—a meek, frail-looking woman, very natural, makeup free, and nothing like the grand diva I had

envisioned. We shook hands and she sat behind her desk. As she leaned forward to speak, the wide-necked sweater she was wearing fell off her shoulder as though it were intentional. She paused a moment, staring at me, then proceeded to ask questions.

She wanted to know my cooking past, where I had worked, and for whom. After about ten minutes, she pointed her long finger at me and said, "Are you sure you're not trying to get in the record business? You don't really look like a chef." The question took me by surprise, and I assured her I knew what I was doing, but I don't think she believed me, not at that moment. Nonetheless, the interview continued for an hour, and I heard all about her favorite foods, her health concerns, her struggle with cholesterol, and a detailed list of what she disliked.

At the end of the hour, Barbra suggested I prepare an "audition" meal for her and some friends the following evening. The next morning, after a run through the grocery store, I worked all afternoon and served them a seafood risotto, a specialty of Liguria, Italy, where I spent many months during my *stage*. For dessert, it was crispy plum strudel, dripping with sweet, red plums and cinnamon.

After dinner, Barbra pushed the kitchen door open, stuck her head in, and said to me, "That was superb. You're hired—but don't you ever cook that way again for me."

And that was it. I started the following morning.

Life now handed me the unexpected challenge of cooking lunch and dinner every day, and often dinner parties on weekends, for a perfectionist who loved to eat like royalty but was mindful about not gaining an ounce. The irony in this situation was that I had just left Italy and France, where no one cared about calories, fats, carbs, or macrobiotics. Instead, to them, it was the *experience* of eating that mattered. It was not necessarily the catch of *scampi* found at a market that morning and thrown on a grill, or perhaps four perfect artichokes clipped and stuffed with bread, garlic, and Parmesan. To them, with whom you share your meal is as important as what you are eating.

I soon learned Barbra rarely left her home. She deeply feared going out, which was understandable since the public always swarmed her. So instead, friends and business associates went to her, and I cooked for them. Every day it was lunch for six, then dinner for ten, or lunch for two and dinner for twelve. Weekends were often larger gatherings, and the dinners lasted late into the night. It was truly grueling, but I was young—everything's so much easier when you're young. I literally wore running shoes and I sprinted through the grocery store, pushing my cart and tossing in items as I ran, like that game show we've all seen. The foods I was preparing were exciting to me. It was the eighties, and I was captivated by a new "California" approach to cooking, with my finger on an endless supply of unique and super-fresh ingredients, a style that passionately influenced my cooking.

There were a few unspoken rules around the house, number one of which was made very clear to me from the beginning—whatever Barbra wants, Barbra gets.

Period.

I could have every vegetable you could think of in the refrigerator except broccoli and if she wanted broccoli, I had to go get broccoli. It was how we all operated: me, the housekeepers, the secretaries, the gardeners, everyone. Often, Barbra would call me at home early in the morning when I was still asleep in bed. These were in the days before we had caller ID, but as the phone rang and woke me up, I always knew it was her. I'd lay there in my sleepy daze and listen to her tell me about a new diet or way of eating she heard about from a friend, and how she wanted to begin it immediately, with lunch. So, sure enough, I'd dash through a grocery store to get precisely what she wanted. Once, I remember preparing her a salad for lunch when her assistant came barreling into the kitchen and blurted, "Barbra wants a Swanson's fried chicken TV dinner. Go get one. And make sure it's Swanson's." Then she ran out.

Huh? Are you serious?

Three grocery stores later, I found the TV dinner,

rushed home, heated it up, and then, in an epic fail, transferred the chicken, the mashed potatoes, the green beans, and the gravy to a dinner plate and sent it up the dumbwaiter from the kitchen to her bedroom. Thirty seconds later, it came back down to the kitchen with a quickly scribbled note that said, "Why isn't it in the foil tray?!" I grabbed the tray, put everything back in its little compartments, and sent it back to her.

And so I learned—just give her what she wanted.

I had been hearing about "the ranch" from my very first days. The ranch was a sprawling property, many beautiful acres of Mediterranean brush, that Barbra bought on a mountainside deep in Malibu. The grounds had views of the ocean and were serene, peaceful, and very private. Mostly on weekends, Barbra and her staff would head to the ranch where she usually invited friends and business associates to dinner and to perhaps spend the night. It was not easy to find the estate, and there were a series of coded gates one would need to access and a security guard stationed at the final stop. Having worked for Barbra just two weeks, she told me she was planning a dinner party for a small group and wanted to have it at the ranch the following weekend. We planned the event, and that Saturday morning, I loaded my car with a bunch of stuff, stopped off at the grocery store, and was off to Malibu. Anxious, I hadn't slept the night before.

When I arrived, the security guard opened the main gate, and I slowly drove in. The first thing I noticed was that everything instantly changed—the pavement, trees, detailed landscaping, everything, suddenly transformed into a beautiful, controlled perfection, as though I had entered Disneyland. There were flowers everywhere and a trickling brook that flowed along the main road. I later learned that the brook was artificial, controlled with pumps that had to be turned on, and was just one more element in the grand design of the property. As I drove along and took in the surroundings, I passed tennis courts and a pavilion where Barbra would frequently have lunch, and I caught my first glimpse of the pink golf cart she used to get around.

Years earlier when Barbra purchased the estate, she built her first house there, which everyone referred to as "the ranch house," a large, rectangular building, sort of hacienda-like with lots of wood beams and throw blankets and a great, central fireplace. This was her main home, and it was there she'd have most of the dinner parties. As I pulled into the main driveway, I was met by her assistant who took me to the kitchen and then told me to follow her for a tour of the rest of the property. What I was about to see would defy description.

A paved pathway, the width of the golf cart, led around the landscape to unveil another home. This home was built in a completely different style, literally into the face of a mountainside, three-stories vertical, and had been dubbed "the mountain house." As we entered the front door, it opened to a small, cave-like room with natural-cut stone walls, a seating area, a small kitchen, and an elevator. It felt as though it had been chiseled out of the mountain—truly remarkable. Up on the second floor, off the bedroom, was a spa-like, vast, walk-in bath that resembled a hidden cave you'd stumble upon on a tropical island, filled with lush plants, waterfalls dripping down the stone walls, and beams of natural light everywhere. I had never seen anything like this before. The third floor was a huge, projector theater with large, comfy sofas and chairs where she and her guests would frequently watch films.

As we continued on our path, we came to a third house, "the tree house," named for the large, hundred-year-old tree that grew up through its center. This house was literally built around the tree and had a distinctive Santa Fe pueblo feel, with adobe exteriors, plastered walls, carved wooden doors, and earthy hues. Everything looked as though it was set to be photographed by *Architectural Digest*. Walking out the back door and along the path, I noticed that the path changed abruptly from natural stone pavers to a distinctive pattern of geometrically cut colored tiles in four colors--black, silver, red, and pink. This tiled path continued around the hillside and led to, yes, another home. Parked in the driveway was a pink 1949 Cadillac Coup de Ville, the first of hundreds of decorative items that adorned the home. Opening the large, black-lacquered front door revealed a remarkable testament to art deco design and style. The "deco house" was museum-like and was more for display than practical use. The four-colored scheme of the pathway continued to run through the house, and everything in the interior— absolutely everything, including the appliances and the *interior* of the refrigerator—were custom painted to match precisely. Even the hundred pairs of unused heels that Barbra had lined on shelves in a walk-in closet matched one of the four colors: top shelf all silver, then a shelf of black, then red, then pink. Every accessory was antique and authentic and insanely expensive. I was warned that no one could touch anything.

It was getting late and we headed back to the main house where I began to prepare dinner. At 5:00 p.m., Barbra's assistant, who, by the way, was and still is a lifelong, devoted employee with an almost religious devotion to Barbra and who has remarkable energy, came rushing into the kitchen and told me it was time to turn on the lights. Every afternoon, precisely at five, we would run throughout the property, and all the houses, and turn on every single light—and there were hundreds, including the brook. And, at the same time, we would light a hundred candles, all strategically placed.

A short time later, with the stage set, Barbra's friends arrived. As it turned out, I later learned that this particular dinner party was quite important to her. I was told to cook for twelve people but thirteen showed up. This did not make Barbra happy and, in a panic, her assistant re-set the table. From a chef's point of view, adding one person more is generally *not* an issue—but, I had prepared homemade pasta with Bolognese meat sauce as a first course and I knew there was barely enough for twelve. Among the guests was a very well-known celebrity who brought his young girlfriend, a waif of a girl who never said a word. At dinner time, I divided the pasta among thirteen plates and served it to the guests. As I laid the pasta in front of the girlfriend, she turned to me and said, "Oh, I'm vegetarian. No meat." I froze and just stared at her. Barbra, who always knew everything that was going on in the room, looked over with a pissed-off smirk and said, "Just give her pasta with plain tomato sauce." As I smiled and calmly returned to the kitchen, I thought, *Where the fuck am I supposed to get that?!* I absolutely knew there was not an extra strand of pasta, and I certainly did not have meatless sauce. In an adrenaline-fueled panic, I filled the sink with hot water, grabbed the pasta off the plate, and agitated it clean in the water, like I was washing a dirty towel. I pulled the pasta out of the sink, piled it on a plate, and turned to the meat sauce. I thought for a moment, grabbed a strainer, dumped in the meat sauce, and shook it madly, straining out every little bit of meat—voilà, tomato sauce. I spooned it on the pasta, ran to the kitchen door, stopped, took a breath, and slowly entered the dining room. The girlfriend smiled and said thank you. Barbra made eye contact with me and grinned like Mona Lisa. I swear she knew what I had done.

She always knew.

What is most fascinating about a celebrity of this grandeur is the lack of familiarity with life's daily tasks that the rest of us must endure, such as going to the bank, or to the post office, or trying to find a parking space, or waiting for your turn to use a piece of equipment at a public gym, or even going to a grocery store. This became quite evident to me late one afternoon as Barbra and I chatted about a dinner party for twelve she had planned for the following night. Earlier that day, I had made her a grilled chicken breast for lunch and she really liked it.

I said to her, "Is there anything special you'd like for the party?"

She replied, "Too bad you can't make that chicken breast I had for lunch."

"Well, I can," I said.

She said abruptly, "Well, if you buy twelve chickens for the breasts, what are you going to do with the rest of the chicken?"

I just stared at her for a moment.

I said, "Ah, you can buy just breasts. You don't have to buy whole chickens."

Now she just stared at me.

She had no idea that chicken was sold cut-up in the grocery store. She had not been to a grocery store probably since her teens in Brooklyn.

"Really?" she said. "And you can get just legs, or just wings, too??"

Thus, the secluded life of this great superstar. And frankly, I didn't blame her for not going out, since when she did—and I was there to attest to it—she was mobbed. Everyone wanted to see her, meet her, take a picture with her, and tell her how much they loved her. When I finished at the end of the day and drove off the property, crowds of fans were always gathered outside the gate with their cameras and snapped pictures of *me*, just by chance I could be with Barbra.

After I stopped working for Barbra to open my own restaurant, she called one evening and told me she was just leaving the studio and wanted to stop by my new place for dinner. "Of course," I told her, "I'll have a table waiting for you." I was so excited. When she arrived, her floppy hat was pulled down over her head and, in the dark entry of the restaurant, you really couldn't tell who it was, but it was Barbra—I remembered her walk and her frame. We hugged a moment, and I knew to get her to the table fast. As she sat, I told her I'd be back in a few minutes to suggest what to order. She smiled, and I walked away. From the back of the restaurant, I looked across the dining room and saw three people were already at her table. After a minute, they walked away, and I went into the kitchen. When I came out, four other people were at her table, and while they stood there, another woman walked to the table. As I headed overs to talk about the menu, two other people had stood and beat me there. I heard them say, "Oh my God, we love you." With that, Barbra smacked her hand on the table and shouted, "I need my privacy, too!" I pushed myself in front of them and they all walked away. I apologized to Barbra that this was happening, but she said nothing. She was clearly upset. I said, "Let me make you something I know you'll like," and she said, "Fine." I went back into the kitchen and told my food expeditor, a big guy, to stand like security in the dining room and not let anyone near her table, which he promptly did and discreetly kept people at bay. She had dinner, hugged me goodbye, and scurried away. Sometimes celebrities like attention, and other times they don't.

During my time with her, I received many letters, phone calls, and interview requests asking me what she was like. People actually sent me recorded tapes of songs they had written in hopes that I would pass them along to her to potentially record. Even people from high school with whom I had lost contact many years earlier tracked me down with questions. The elaborate security system and high walls she had around her property were necessary since there was always a fair share of fanatics and obsessive fans lurking around.

Most difficult for me was the awkwardness I sometimes felt just being there in her home, always present, from early in the morning when she'd wake up and slouch into the kitchen for tea, until late at night when she'd pick through the refrigerator for a snack. There's a sense of intrusion that comes with the territory, for having so much staff in your home, and it was uneasy at times for both me and her. I was always there when something went wrong, and Barbra would yell and curse like a sailor, or when she would argue with a family member or a boyfriend. Many times, I would just go outside for a while to give her privacy.

With time, I became quite relaxed in her presence. It was as though a friend would come into the kitchen wearing sweats and a T-shirt, drawn in by the wonderful smell of what I had cooking on the stove, or she and I would chat a while about something in her yard or by the pool. But then, there were times, on those rare and special occasions, when she was heading to a major event, or an award ceremony, that I'd see her in full, evening makeup, dressed in a sparkling gown, hair coiffed and perfect, that my voice would tremble with nervousness as I spoke, as though she were a different person, that grand diva we all admired and applauded.

People often asked me what she was really like, and they still do, and want to know if her reputation of being a ballbuster was genuine. Well, it was, but being around her, you appreciate why. I used to think of her as chairman of the board—the five phone lines in the home were constantly ringing, and all calls were for her. Everything she did had to do with her career and there seemed to be little downtime. She didn't have an attorney, she had a law firm, and it was big business. She rarely seemed to laugh but instead would just say, "That's funny," and believe me, when she was pissed, well, you'd better stand clear. And she absolutely loathed being called Babs and would most certainly let you know so.

There's an intriguing combination of wealth and celebrity that many like Barbra use to get what they want. A glorious example unfolded before my eyes on the birthday of her then-boyfriend. As a surprise, she decided to redo his "room," an area on the second floor that he used as an office, and gym. There was talk about what was going to happen on this day for quite a while, and on the morning of his birthday, as he unsuspectingly left for work, there was an unusual stillness in the house. Then, the moment he drove away, it started. Barbra, as only she could do because of who she was, coordinated the services of fifty people—designers, plumbers, electricians, carpet layers, painters, and furniture delivery companies, who, in an eight-hour window, and through massive planning, managed to completely demolish and rebuild his room. All the trades came at precise times, one literally standing outside waiting for another to finish before they would begin their part. By the end of the workday, she had coordinated the removal of an existing bathroom and completely rebuilt a new one, including new tile, fixtures, toilet, and a steam shower. Carpet was replaced, everything was repainted, doors were replaced, window treatments were added, exercise equipment was delivered, and a full wall was mirrored. Office furniture arrived late afternoon, just as the phone company was completing the phone installation and a florist showed up with a few bunches of flowers to finish it off. Through it all, I could hear Barbra calmly but quite sternly directing everyone. The remodeled room was spectacular down to the new monogramed gold pen that stood proudly in its holder on the desk. When her boyfriend came home at the end of the day, Barbra met him at the door and the two of them walked up the stairs together. It was a brilliant demonstration of a most special privilege and talent she had.

But I must tell you that when I first heard her sing in front of me, it was haunting. As she rehearsed one afternoon with her accompanist, standing next to that white piano, her hands in the back pockets of her jeans, relaxed, almost possessed, the sound that filled the room and the lush resonance of her voice was something I had never heard before. In an instant, I understood her gift. It became beautifully apparent.

I remember how irritated she once was that a record company was giving her a hard time about an album she wanted to make, something they said was outside the realm of popularity at the time. In the kitchen one afternoon, she told me, "You know, I've made dozens of records for them and you'd think they'd trust me by now." But she pushed back and ultimately recorded what became one of her most successful and defining works, *The Broadway Album*. While recording, she called me one morning and asked me to drop off her lunch at the studio. When I arrived, I made my way to a room of musicians, a full orchestra, quietly sitting at their stands, all staring at Barbra, who had just walked over to her microphone. She had on a coarsely knit floppy sweater, which didn't surprise me since she was always chilled, and had a cup of hot lemon water in her hand. I silently stood in the back, completely still, as though I were about to witness a once-in-a-lifetime event. My heart nervously pounded as she pulled on headphones, leaned into the mic, and said, "Let's try one." With that, the conductor nodded yes, raised his baton, and cued the orchestra to begin. For the next four minutes, Barbra sang, and I thought, *God, how perfect*—effortless and controlled, flowing with the swells of the orchestra as they all became louder and softer, Barbra sort of conducting everyone with her arm as she sung, until her final soft, lingering note. With that, she looked up and seemed to snap back from wherever she was. She immediately started calling out change after change to the conductor, specific moments that the strings were too loud, or the horns were too soft, or the tempo was off. The conductor scribbled notes as fast as he could, trying to keep up with her, and at times seemed to turn his head, surprised by her comments, but never said a word. This went on for twenty minutes. Then, she giggled about something and said, "Okay, let's try it again."

Barbra's assistant told me once that Barbra could hear things in music that other people couldn't, which became quite apparent to me as she replayed these soundtracks in her home. From morning to night, I could hear her replay a song, starting and stopping, and starting and stopping, rewinding, replaying—from the kitchen I could hear her, obsessed with perfection, and it would go on for weeks as she edited her songs. She carries this great intensity in so many aspects of her life, from recording, to interior design, to food, and it left me with an enlightened awareness and with many glorious memories. I would not trade them for anything.

Nothing delights a chef more than cooking for someone who appreciates what they do.

As my time passed with Barbra, a rumbling to follow my path and open my own restaurant was stirring inside of me. I was twenty-eight. I was ready.

I believe, eventually, we end up where we're supposed to be. I met a young couple who were searching for a chef for their first venture and the three of us collaborated and opened a small Los Angeles bistro. My menu took on this newly learned California style of cooking—light, clean, healthy, and tasty, but I added an international spin with Thai foods, Indian curries, and indulgences such as sea bass baked Yucatán-style in banana leaves layered with garlic, orange slices, and *achiote*. We served large portions, emphasizing the grill, and featured those novel California pizzas, with toppings like grilled salmon and brie or grilled eggplant and goat cheese, a far cry from the New York marinara and mozzarella pie.

The restaurant was a hit, and we could barely keep up with it; we would turn a table four times on a Saturday night. Good bread was hard to find so I decided to bake my own from a recipe I learned in Italy—a crusty boule scented with rosemary, garlic, and onion—and its popularity spawned a new venture, a large wholesale bakery that I opened just up the street.

Over the next decade, my passion turned to bread.

There is just something about baking a living dough that intrigues me. It seems an unassuming process, but it is riddled with complexities and variables, like winemaking, all of which subtly affects what you get when you pull the loaves out of the oven—humidity, temperature, time, taste of the water, or even the amount of gluten in the flour. And let me tell you, baking a loaf of bread at home is an entirely different experience than producing thousands of pounds of dough with hydraulic kneading machines, rotating deck ovens, and teams of bakers and packaging people. The folks employed in a commercial bakery work their asses off. It is a twenty-four-hour day of heat and sweat. Soon, I branched out to muffins, pastries, cookies, and just about everything else a bakery could produce, and opened three retail coffee shops in high-maintenance Los Angeles to sell my goods. It all became quite successful.

But something was missing. I wanted to cook. That's what I was meant to do.

After nine years of baking, I sold the operation and headed back to the professional kitchen. I opened a big, exciting Los Angeles restaurant and dove headfirst into the pool of editorial critics and public relation snobs that one must appease to have any sort of success in that city. By default, with celebrities, tourists, and scores of new faces passing through the dining room every night, it kept me busier than I could have possibly hoped. But through a sordid turn of events, after six years, I sold the restaurant and I moved on.

Within just a month, as often happens with restauranteurs, an idea sparked, and I did it again. This time, it was a diner—a hip, fifties burger joint with bottled sodas, hand-cut fries, and chocolate malts. The place opened at 6:00 a.m. for breakfast and closed at 11:00 p.m., every single day of the week—day after day after day. It was a relentless staffing nightmare and never stopped.

I was tired. I needed to be rebooted, like my computer, so things worked properly again. The operational side of running businesses in Los Angeles, a city where everything is uphill, had taken its punishing toll. Life had become stale, and once again, I sold.

This time I packed my bags.

I landed in Palm Springs, a haven for me over the years whenever I needed downtime. I soon learned that this peaceful little resort, a private playground for many since the 1930s, was in desperate need of a place for people to socialize and eat. A really cool, modish restaurant with sensational food just did not exist, and a new population was growing—countless realtors and developers and a younger generation wanting a more laid-back lifestyle were relocating to quiet, charming

Palm Springs. The stifling hot summers used to leave Palm Springs desolate, but now there was traffic in August. Everyone I met said, "Yeah, I just moved here."

Once again, I was in the right place at the right time.

At the post office one morning, I noticed an old abandoned building sitting quietly across the street. It had no windows, a sealed metal front door, dead landscaping, and a small FOR LEASE sign in the front. I had no idea what it used to be. I walked around back and saw a large concrete slab mounted with old oil compressors and piles of metal parts strewn everywhere. The middle section of the building had no roof, letting a steady wind of hot desert sand gust through day and night.

I thought, *This is a perfect building for a restaurant.*

That afternoon, I called the realtor on the sign and asked my first question: "Is it zoned for restaurant use?" Her one-word answer of yes was all it took to begin the journey of a brand-new restaurant. And it happened again.

But this time was different.

Missing now were those hind legs of the big city that kept kicking me in the face. Gone were the callous, professional critics and the games I had to play to be considered a player. There was no surge of anonymous, faceless customers flowing in and out of the dining room every night. Instead, this time, I knew people's names. I knew what they did. I knew what they liked to eat and how many children they had. This time, the staff enjoyed working there and did not quit and move on after a month. We all became friends and family. There was time to travel again and to eat other people's food, and I could rest assured that while I was gone, my staff would have my back. At last, I had the glorious feeling of finding home.

ASS KISSING

"Life is fraught with opportunities
to keep your mouth shut."

WINSTON CHURCHILL

I went to a city office with questions about the host of permits required to open a restaurant and to courteously introduce myself and my project. I had a six-inch-thick roll of architectural plans under my arm and a detailed prospectus iteming costs, projections, and the like. When I told the lead official my intentions to open a big, new restaurant, built from the ground up in an underdeveloped remote area, he looked over his glasses at me, shook his head, and snubbed, "Have you ever done this before?" What I thought was, *What a dumbass*

RUNNING THROUGH THE SWINGING DOORS

question—it's really none of your business, but instead, in what has become a never-ending effort to suck up to people, I humbly nodded, "Yes, sir."

The process of opening a restaurant is much like spending a year chained up in a cell of the Tower of London. The torture begins the moment you attempt to raise capital for the project. After spending months putting together a written prospectus, the detailed script of your vision, the story of the food and menu, how the restaurant will feel, who it will attract, who is the competition, financial projections, cost analyses, etc., you must begin to sell your story to potential investors and humiliatingly beg for money. It helps if you have some cash of your own in the pot—if you don't invest in yourself, it's hard to ask others, and you must make it very clear to them exactly what they will receive in return for taking the astronomical and frankly stupid risk of investing in a restaurant. Statistically, they will lose everything and end up wasting a lot of money just to guarantee a prime reservation or a little VIP treatment when they dine.

Understanding why someone agrees to make such a daring investment helps you pick your targets. Obviously, investors are the rich, and they will most often just write you a check for their contribution. They are the sort who love to eat and love to dine and have a good time, and I believe, deep down inside, are sideline restaurateurs themselves, often spilling with unsolicited comments and design opinions that you must endure. Once you sign up the first one, the others follow more easily. Often, an investor is the best source of finding other investors; they enthusiastically sell the project to their friends and convince them to get in on the deal. Ultimately, they invest in you as a person, and if you believe in yourself, and trust yourself, they will believe in you, as well.

What excites an investor most is the uncertainty of the future.

Fundraising often must extend even beyond the grand opening due to the likelihood of the project landing way the hell over budget—everything always, without exception, costs more than you think it will, and you are incessantly plagued with unexpected expenses. But at one point, with some capital in the bank, and more promisingly heading your way, you must begin building. The gate is open. It is time to run.

My first hurdle is tapdancing around the counter clerks in the city office in my attempt to get them to pound their precious red stamp on plans that gives me the legal "go" to start building. And for the record, city offices, and I don't care where you are in the country, run the same. It's like the same people work in all of them. Usually, they do not accept appointments, and if I ask when a specific inspector will be there, no one ever knows. I cannot phone them, because when I do, I have to leave a message and, of course, no one ever calls me back. If I'm lucky, maybe I hear back two days later.

So, my morning is dedicated to sitting on a bench with a band of architects, designers, contractors, and anxious business owners, all waiting to be called to plead their case. God forbid there is ever a sense of urgency. The clerks walk around sluggishly, seemingly bored or pissed off that they have to work such a shitty job, with either a smug, carefree arrogance or just simply bewildered and confused. They know they have the power to impart their blessing on your project with permit *approval* or send it down into a frustrating spiral of corrections, adjustments, and lots of unnecessary expense.

Dad would say, "They got you by the balls."

To a business owner, especially in the beginning, everything is about money, and I know for damn sure the last thing city people care about or I should ever mention is how much something is going to cost. As they study my plans, they will likely walk away a few times to reference the great city bible—the codebook. I am left standing there, dripping sweat under my shirt, until they come back and inevitably mumble that something is not "to code." What I hear is something like: "You'll have to redesign this entire area because Section 34.5 requires a wheelchair ramp up the side of the room and around the corner with a dedicated pathway to the parking lot and an eight-foot landing with extended guardrails because you can only raise so many feet per liner foot. Have your architect redraw the plans and submit back three copies for re-check."

Then they just stand there and look at you.

I think to myself, *I'm fucked*.

And I am.

If you live in a small town, this maddening process is made even worse because these small city offices do not have in-house engineers and architects to review the plans. Instead, they mail them to other cities where teams of unseen henchmen dissect every detail and make sidenotes they unsympathetically call "corrections."

When it is all finished, usually many weeks later, my plans are returned to me with an attached list of these corrections. I cannot ask questions; I must comply. If I did want to inquire if they could override a correction, even something simple, I must fill out forms they call "variances," submit them back into the system, pay more fees, wait more weeks, resubmit, wait more, redraw the plan, wait more, then wait more, then wait more. By the time it's finished, I have made concessions that just suck, I am already overbudget, the design is very different than my original plan, and I hate everyone. Now it's time to pay the terrifying list of permitting fees, which are always much more than originally budgeted, and finally—finally—they pound that cherished, red stamp on my set of plans that gives me legal permission to build.

The worst of the process always seems to be the rules regarding disabled access. In every facility I have ever designed, it is an epic task to comply with the over-written and tedious codebook of regulations that was established by Congress in 1990 called the Americans with Disabilities Act. If you read it, a big section is dedicated just to the fines and potential lawsuits for business owners who do not obey the rules. It even includes a list of attorneys that the public can notify if a business does not comply. Everything has to be the right height or width or level and *everywhere* in your facility must have equal access to someone in a wheelchair.

So, for example, if half of the dining room is raised one step and the other half is ground level, that would be illegal, because a wheelchair must have access to *all* areas, not designated areas. You would need a ramp to provide equal access to the whole room, for everyone.

Okay, I get it.

It's a good thing to make it easier for chair-bound customers to get around, but the law is way overworked (big surprise) and the inspectors never budge and certainly never choose to use common sense. They pace around with measuring tapes, notebooks, and cameras as they write up all the violations, smirking a little when they find something.

I recall once in Los Angeles, the ADA inspector, a man who spoke English like he just got off a plane from another part of the world, comes to do the final inspection just a week before I had hoped to open. His accent is so thick, I can't understand him. I ask him to repeat everything he says to me. As he does the inspection, finally, I say, "I'm sorry, sir, I just can't understand what you're saying." He turns to look at me, raises his arm, and blurts, "I don't have time to repeat everything to you!"

Well, okay then.

I back down, because I know, and he knows, that he has the power to destroy me and my hopes of opening anytime soon.

After the next forty-five minutes, as he and I do the inspection immersed in our newly found silence, this guy heads to the ladies' room, me quietly following behind him like a donkey on a rope, and again he starts measuring things. He bends down and measures the distance from the side rim of a toilet to the wall. By code, it had to be at least seventeen inches. He says nothing and writes in his notebook.

When he finishes his inspection, he tells me I failed. According to this imbecile's *written report*, the toilet was sixteen and three-quarter inches from the wall, not seventeen. A quarter of a fucking inch short.

I actually have to call a plumber to remove the toilet, break the tile and the concrete, cut and reset a drainpipe, reset the toilet, recement, and retile. He comes back a week later, measures again, signs the inspection card that we passed, drops it on the table, and leaves without saying a word.

Maybe it's the frustration of having to correct things for a living, like a jaded schoolteacher grading papers all afternoon, or maybe it's just a sad side of human nature, but I learned a long time ago that no matter how much you design to code and pay strict attention to detail, when the ADA inspector enters your facility at the end of construction, when your stress level is maxed out and you're desperate to open, they always find some frivolous violation that sets you back—often, way back.

I took on the construction of a nightclub years ago. It was designed with a small, elevated stage next to the dance floor where the DJ would spin. It had four steps up and was built as originally drawn on the *approved* plans submitted to the city—those that displayed the big, red stamp. During a final inspection, the ADA inspector, a man in a wheelchair himself, rolls up to the stage and says, "How is a DJ in a chair supposed to get up there?"

I just stare at him.

I have no idea what to say.

I *want* to say, *We'll carry him*, but I know he would not find that as funny as I do.

Instead, I say, "Our DJ isn't in a chair. I've already hired him," and he responds, "Well, someday you may hire one who is. You need a ramp or an elevator chairlift."

Huh?!

A ramp? An elevator chairlift??

Then he says, "And, if you build a ramp for the height of four steps, it would have to be ten feet long."

I say, "But a ten-foot-long ramp would extend through the middle of the dance floor—you can't have a ramp in the dance floor. There's got to be another way."

He says, "Well, you can always install an elevator chairlift on the other side of the stage."

Now I am getting pissed and explain to him that the *city-approved plans* clearly show an elevated stage and DJ booth and does *not* require a ramp or elevator. He tells me he's not sure know how that happened, but he would not sign off on the permit allowing us to open until we comply.

And he leaves.

As it turns out, opening day is scheduled just a week away but is delayed more than a month because I have to find and purchase a wheelchair elevator lift for $26,000, pay for the installation and re-construction of the backstage area that cost another $3,000, remove permanently mounted bar stools for access, pay an electrician $2,500 for dedicated wiring, and have it re-inspected by a California sanctioned inspection company for $650—all before I could call the inspector to come back.

When he returns and sees what I did, he says, "Okay, good."

He signs the final inspection card and rolls away.

And you guessed it—during the many years that followed, the elevator chairlift was never used once. Never. It sat there, a dusty waste of time and money.

Money means nothing to city planners and the F-troop of construction inspectors, and they get really irritated if I ever cry that a required change would cost too much. It does not matter to them in the least. Every little smidgeon of detail in the buildout must be in compliance with some line item in the codebook—it's the only way they are legally protected if a disaster happens. If I find a fabulous light fixture in an antique store, I can legally hang it at home, but if it does not have a UL safety listing, for example, I cannot hang it in a restaurant; it could potentially burn. It's okay to burn down your house but not your restaurant. Much makes no sense.

The battery from inspectors continues for the duration of the construction project. Every on-site inspection is stressful and nerve-racking unless, of course, I can successfully manage to become buds with the inspector. Sometimes it happens—maybe we worked together on another project, or we used to live in the same town, or maybe he is just retired contractor who has been the victim of inspectors himself before and knows the rap.

But most often, the city building inspector walks onto the job site like a boxer entering the ring for a fight. They huff around formidable, over-the-top critical, and they do not want to be talked to or brown-nosed. They have the power to eat me. Through the course of the building process, from day one to the final inspection, there likely may be twenty-five inspections by the same guy, many of which you fail, and some of which you must return to the city to plead your case to department heads. By the end, I never want to see any of these people again.

And don't think for a moment that the onslaught of inspectors ceases when you open. They continue to bestow panic on you for years to come, inspecting updraft systems, sewer lines and grease traps, work safety hazards, fire prevention systems, and the most dreaded of them all, the one who could potentially wreck my business for months, is the terrifying health department inspector.

The tales of what has transpired to me during health department inspections over decades could alone fill this book, but know this: These people have the power to surprise visit you, walk around quiet and stoic, write up a report, and close down your operation. What is most unfortunate is that the general public thinks that a B health rating, or worse yet a C, means your kitchen is likely the scene of cockroaches crawling around over warm, raw chicken. Well, that's not necessarily the case, and a bad score can be the result of many things that have nothing to do with food or cleanliness.

When the inspector shows up, it is always at the worst time. It's when I am busiest, behind schedule, or shorthanded. They like to surprise their prey and usually just ambush the kitchen with a clipboard, pen light, thermometer, and a camera, making sure no one has time to make last-minute adjustments. At this point, I know not to speak—instead, I usually just follow along and answer questions, acting cool and nonchalant. What I know is that these inspectors seem to assess the situation and make the number of violations fit a preconceived score in their head. Now, I'm quite sure they would deny this, but I have seen it. They could easily find fifty violations if they want, just as a traffic cop could pull over a car every minute for some reason if they want, but instead, they always seem to write up the perfect number of violations to fit the score that they *feel* is appropriate, making some violations stick and letting others slide. When they leave, I smile, escort them to the door, thank them, and assure them any violations I have will be addressed. As I turn around, I look up and think, *Fuck—thank God that's over.*

At 4:45 p.m., on a hot, Friday afternoon at an L.A. restaurant I owned years ago, the phone is ringing call after call, the kitchen is pushing through its usual pre-dinner bedlam, bussers are running around stocking bus stations with silver and glassware, and servers are in the restrooms fixing their hair and makeup—a typical scenario—hundreds of reservations on the books, we are just about to open the door. As I chat with a cook in the kitchen, the back-kitchen door opens and slowly enters a young woman. She looks sort of Asian, maybe Pilipino, thick, black-rimmed glasses, and held a clipboard. As she approaches me, I notice a lanyard around her neck identifying her as a health department inspector. Here we go.

"I'm here to do your health inspection," she says.

"Ah, okay. We're just about to open," I say. "Where would you like to begin?"

"I will take care of it—you don't have walk with me," she blurts with arrogance.

"Okay then. I'm here if you need me."

She disappears into the chaos of cooks hustling to get ready for service, but at no time does she leave my sight—I know exactly where she is, what she's looking at, who she's talking to, everything. How much she writes, or doesn't write, on her clipboard tells me how we're doing. A half hour later, she finds me and says, "Take me to your water heater?" In the decades I have endured these inspections, no one has ever asked me that. They certainly check hot water temperature, but no one ever cared where the tank was.

"Ah, it's outside, along the alley in the corridor next to us," I say.

"Okay, let me see," she says.

So, she and I head outside the back-kitchen door to the alley and we walk to a corridor about thirty feet from the kitchen door. Down the corridor between the restaurant and the neighboring business is a locked doorway where the heater is located. When we arrive, I open the door with my key. As I do, she pushes in front of me, turns on her flashlight, and scans around the dark room—up the walls, down the walls, and around the base of the tank. Suddenly, a lone cockroach zips up the wall, running from the light.

"Oh, oh!" she says.

I think, *It's just a cockroach.*

She gets behind the water tank and continues to beam the light around the little room. Moments later, a second cockroach runs by and quickly disappears.

"Oh my! You have an infestation of cockroaches!" she blurts.

"There are just two cockroaches. It's not an infestation," I answer.

64

"More than one cockroach indicates an infestation. You must close this restaurant immediately."

It has never been easy for me to hold my tongue, but one thing I learned at a young age is you do not give shit to the cops, to your boss, or to an inspector. If you do, you lose.

I said, "I have 250 reservations tonight. I can have a pest guy here in the morning to spray—you can't close me down now."

"Yes, I can. You have an infestation, and you are in violation. You must close."

My voice gets firmer: "I'm not closing the restaurant. This is stupid. There are two cockroaches in a room far from the kitchen, and you want to shut me down on a Friday night."

"I am ordering you to close. If you do not, I will phone my supervisors," she shouts.

This goes back and forth a few times until I finally say, "I don't care who you call—just get out of here."

With that, I close the water heater room door, and as she and I walk back to the restaurant, in my rage and frustration, I mumble *What a bitch* to myself. She gets in her car, which was parked in the alley, and I go back inside the restaurant.

I know she's not done with this.

I head to my hostess and my manager and say, "We have to close tonight. She's closing the restaurant. We have to call everyone and tell them we're having a plumbing issue and have to close."

And we do just that.

My hostess calls 70 reservations, about 250 people, and cancels them. I tell the cooks to break down the kitchen, trying to salvage as much as possible, but sauces can be heated only once; many are tossed out. Bussers have to break down all the tables and, along with the servers, they head home with no tips from the night. It's now a little after 6:00 p.m. and cooks are gone. As I finish in the kitchen, my hostess comes up to me and tells me the police are in the dining room. I walk through the swinging doors into a room of six police officers and six other men with health department lanyards around their necks. Twelve men.

"Can I help you?" I say.

A health department guy says to me in broken English, "You must cease operation."

"Obviously, I have. There's no one here. I canceled the evening," I said.

"You may not reopen until this facility passes a reinspection. If you do, you will be arrested."

I try to explain to this guy what had happened, how there were two lone cockroaches in a remote room not even attached to the kitchen, and how his inspector unfairly targeted me. In the middle of my sentence, he turns away, walks to the front door of the restaurant, and posts a large, orange notice stating we are in violation and have been condemned by the health department. He then opens his briefcase and pulls out a big, fat red "C" health rating, replacing the "A" I had always gotten in the past.

"When can I get a reinspection?" I ask.

"Call our offices and schedule an appointment next week."

Everyone now leaves. My hostess stays with me and now cancels all reservations for Saturday and Sunday, and I schedule a bug spray for Monday morning. Then I go home.

Late Monday morning after the spray, I call the health department and am transferred to the department head. I tell him I have a receipt from a pest control company and ask for a reinspection. He tells me I must come to his office to discuss proper sanitation procedures. His first available appointment is Wednesday.

On Wednesday, I take my bug-spray report and head downtown to the busy city offices. When I arrive, it seems like the counter reception lady is expecting me and she tells me to sit and wait. A half hour later, I am escorted to a conference room. When I walk in, seated at a large, round, table are about eight people, including the young original inspector. It looks like a meeting for immigration services—everyone is from somewhere else and has lanyards around their necks with names I can't come close to pronouncing. They are totally silent, staring at me, and are void of any personality whatsoever. For the next *hour*, I sit in this hot, stuffy room, and listen to various people, with incomprehensible accents, explain to me the fundamentals of restaurant sanitation, like the importance of employee handwashing, or holding food at the proper temperatures. Twice my eyes close, and I jerk them open. It's hell.

At one point, I ask when I could reopen. The department head looks at me and blurts back, "Furthermore, if you use profanity again to any of my inspectors, I will close your establishment permanently."

He actually said that.

"You must apologize to her," he demands.

Now, probably more than ever before in my life, I have to do something that I do not want to do. I want to tell her to go F herself, that her insolence and stupidity caused me a week's revenue for no reason, that she has no comprehension of what it's like to own a business, to work long hours, to deal with customers, employees, and inspectors, and to feel the pressure of relying on a steady cash flow for survival.

Instead, I take a deep breath, look at her with the eyes of a murderer, grit my teeth, and slowly say, "I'm sorry I called you a bitch."

No one says anything.

The department head tells me they would reinspect

the restaurant the next morning, Thursday. At the time of the reinspection, three agents come in and spend an hour on their backs under equipment throughout the restaurant—in the kitchen, the dining room, the bathrooms, shining flashlights everywhere and find nothing. When they reinspect the water tank room, sure enough they spot a single, loan cockroach. I fail. They tell me I must re-spray, then they will inspect again. The exterminator returns on Friday morning, but the inspectors cannot return until Monday—I lose another weekend and have to throw away a lot of food that had spoiled by this time.

By the end of the *next* week, I finally pass inspection and am permitted to open again. Even though the original inspector found no other violations in the restaurant other than the cockroach, the health department required the big, red "C" to remain posted at my front door until the next inspection, months away. This becomes a death sentence—few people comfortably eat in a restaurant that displays a "C" rating. Every single guest that now comes to the restaurant has to be put to ease that the dreadful rating has nothing to do with cleanliness or food safety. It gets so bad that I station an employee at the front door next to the red "C", and their sole purpose is to explain the situation and calm people's apprehension. Many customers still walk away when they see the rating.

Almost two months later, I am visited again by a health inspector, a new face I have never seen before. He slowly picks through the facility, writing notes while I'm anxiously peering from the distance, until he sits at a table in the dining room to write his summary report—a typical practice. He never asks to see the water heater room. When he finishes, he stands, walks over to the front door, opens his briefcase, and replaces the red "C" with a big, beautiful blue "A." My punishment is over. They have taught me a lesson.

So, after an arduous year of construction, the building process is coming to a close and the parade of inspectors all make their final visits, sign off, and walk away into the distance. The date for the grand opening has been chosen. A new chapter is beginning in the life of my restaurant.

At this point, a delivery of some sort happens every hour. My cell phone is ringing so often, I can't answer all the calls or even check my messages until later that evening. Things arrive and are often wrong, or they do not fit, or it was supposed to be a different color, or I am missing one of the legs from a table. Vendors get word that I am soon opening and show up at the worst times to make their pitches. There are crates of plates, silverware, kitchen equipment, and glassware stacked everywhere, and the guy who said he would be there in the morning to help put all this stuff away no-shows on me. The carpet installation was supposed to happen but is delayed due to a shipping error, which throws off the booth installation, which throws off the upholsterer's work and then throws off the painters. Prospective employees walk in off the street and drop off résumés, but I don't really like any of them. There is nothing to eat except what's inside a bag from Taco Bell, and I eat it because I am starving. I am exhausted and drained, worried, I haven't slept, my relationship is stressed, and I am broke. The building process is grinding to a tumultuous end.

But—I have achieved my goal. I have successfully built a brand-new facility and I lie in bed at night and dream about taking a cruise to Tahiti.

But guess what?

Now I have to hire staff and run a restaurant.

SOLDIERS

"It is literally true that you can succeed best and quickest by helping others to succeed."

NAPOLEON HILL

The inspectors are thankfully gone, the terrazzo is polished, the refrigeration is running, and I have turned a frenetic construction site into a sensational, sexy, state-of-the-art, food-making and moneymaking machine. I have pulled it off.

Whenever I announce to someone I'm about to open a restaurant, I see their eyes pop and the first thing they always blurt back is, "Oh wow, really? What kind of food?" Unless your menu features a specific, ethnic cuisine like Chinese or Italian, for a chef, this is a question that you just hate to answer.

I am often left standing there saying, "Ah, well, ah, it's . . ."

Instead of asking what kind of food is served, from a chef's point view, one should ask, "Where has the chef worked?" "How old is he?" "Does he have a posse of cooks that he's bringing along with him?"

For publicists and PR people, descriptive cuisine lingo like *Modern American* or *Farm-to-Table* or *California Fusion* just bubbles off their lips and is attached to all advertising media they create—but I don't get it. What the hell does *Farm-to-Table* really mean? Almost everything comes from a farm—vegetables, cows, chickens, eggs, even tiny little organic blueberries, and it all travels the route of food vendors, whether a large commercial company or some peddling, rickety farmer driving an old truck. The notion that a farmer picks his berries one by one and hand delivers them to a chef, who then works with them as jewelers handle diamonds, is nonsense and is saved for a handful of pretentious, chef-driven restaurants; it does not happen, and so many restaurants tout *Farm-to-Table* and other misnomers just to seduce the public into thinking they are eating ingredients that Grandma would have grown in her yard.

But you see, to chefs, food does not really fall into all these nice, defined categories. A good menu will often have a theme, like the repeating melody that flows through a symphony, something that runs through it and ties everything together—but in this modern world, with just about every ingredient you can imagine no further than a phone call away and dropped off at your kitchen door the next morning, menus can feature boundless diversity. A talented chef can prepare anything, as a talented painter can paint anything—it is the *interpretation* that changes—their own panache that sets one apart from the other.

So, it is all about the chef and the menu. It is the genesis of the creative process of a new restaurant. Every decision and every choice in the development of a restaurant is based on the menu—the ambiance, the design of the dining room, the staff you hire, what equipment you need, which vendors you will work with, how the kitchen is laid out—everything—it all comes from the menu. It must be balanced, concise, have something for every palate, must not be food typically prepared at home, and must sound mouth-wateringly delicious. It should make you want to lick the page. The more your devoted guests read on a menu that *sounds* delicious, the more often they are apt to return to try it. Such is the world of menu writing.

But what rouses a chef and provides motivation? How do we decide what to cook? For me, it has always been discovering how other people live and cook and eat.

In my early twenties, I was hungry to learn, and I traveled the world as far as I could. I worked in restaurants for free. I wanted to see how other people cooked. In Europe, after a drive of just a few kilometers in any direction, the culinary world changes. I would discover a different local specialty, another shape of pasta, a new beer to taste, or there'd be different fish in a net. I would move around as often as I could on an unknown path and was a big believer in just winging it.

Years later, when I was older and had real responsibilities, my itinerary became micromanaged for two reasons: First, I did not have as much free time to just aimlessly explore and to get the most out of every moment, and second, I had more money—I would not have to occasionally sleep on an airport floor or in the back seat of a car as I had in the past. These new journeys were more adventure than lush vacation, and lord knows, they were not always comfortable—but, when I returned home, I was always a different person.

Travel changes you. It creates deep-rooted memories.

Sometimes what I see breaks my heart, other times it defies description, like the exhilaration of bustling around Saigon at night on motor scooters with ten thousand others in an organized swarm, zooming through wafts of barbecue smoke as we go. Or during an unexpected Cuban downpour when we huddled together under a tin roof in the middle of a tobacco field and were taught by locals to roll cigars. Or in the mountains of central China when I quietly watched a ninety-year-old woman make tofu on the stone path in front of her home. My eyes teared as I watched her old hands strain the soymilk from urn to urn, separating the soft curds.

I have spent the early morning ankle-deep planting seedlings in a muddy rice paddy, then finished the afternoon with a Vietnamese family who showed me how to make rice pancakes for lunch, quick-fried in fat, rolled with vegetables and herbs, and dipped in pungent fish sauce. You know, you learn a lot about people when you share a meal together. I have hiked deep into the steamy, Tahitian jungle to find a vanilla bean farm where locals grow the vinelike pods, ferment them, then blend them into pastes and extracts. More than a mile before the farm, you could smell the sweet, intoxicating scent. I discovered the special green peppercorns of Cambodia, something I had never heard of, and mountainsides of tiny berries that are carefully handpicked, crushed in a pistil, then stirred with vinegar and other ingredients to make the most amazing pepper sauce I had ever tasted.

The distant Szechuan province of China had always fascinated me, and I had to experience their notorious "hot pot" cooking. There, special tables in restaurants are fitted with metal pots built over gas flames that simmer with a cooking liquid of spices, Szechuan peppercorns, goji berries, and a deadly assortment of powerful local red chilis. Words cannot describe the intensity of the broth—a small drop tasted from the end of my chopstick made me quickly reach for my beer. Making matters worse, the restaurants are humid and stuffy, packed with people, and there is always a feather of cigarette smoke floating around. Without ordering, your table is strewn with platters of raw chicken and other meats, raw meatballs, and mysterious vegetables, and the task is then yours to poach them in the cauldron.

At first, it's fun. As the meatballs float when cooked, I grabbed one with my chopsticks, dipped it in sesame oil mixed with raw, minced garlic, and plopped it in my mouth. We chuckled at how spicy they were, and we reached for our beers. Ten minutes later in a full, dripping sweat, the pain was unbearable. My eyes are blurred with tears, and we all had wet napkins on our heads in pathetic attempts to get through the suffering. At one unexpected moment, my body seemed to relax and accept the pain. I must have arrived at my threshold; the door was open, and I could taste again. To experience the complexities and exotic flavors of these simmering meats and vegetables, and the aromas and intricacies of chilis, seeds, aromatics, and spices that bubbled in the hot pot before me had made my arduous excursion to this remote area in central China worth every moment. I did it, and it was glorious.

The maze of streets in Tokyo are lined with the most wonderful noodle houses in the world. Serving as sort of Japanese fast food, these tiny, family-owned restaurants prepare bowls of ramen that are eaten at counters that often seat no more than a handful of partakers. Day and night, customers stand in the tight, steamy rooms, waiting for their turn to grab a seat and sit for a quick meal. The menus are limited, usually just one item—a family's particular recipe, and you order with a nod of your head. No one really talks. Locals choose which noodle house to visit by who's cooking behind the counter, and it becomes a daily routine in the Tokyo lifestyle. As you walk down the streets and peer into these rooms, all you see are people sitting shoulder to shoulder at the counters, heads down, slurping noodles into their mouths.

With just a day left in this hurried city, I set out to have a last meal at what was reputed to be the best ramen in all of Tokyo. Everyone knew of this place and to the Japanese, it was considered perfection. For a good part of the afternoon, and despite repeated directions, I could not find it. Finally, a kind man on the street, chuckling at my quest, led me around corners and under stairways to a small door. "It is here," he said. The front door had no sign—just a few postings of reviews and awards. I opened the door to find a little room divided by a bar top counter. There were eight stools, three of which were taken. Behind the counter stood a young, handsome man whose head was down chopping something. All I could hear was the faint hum of exhaust and the tapping from his knife on the cutting board. He had just opened, and though I tried to get his attention, he did not look up. Timidly, I sat at a stool. Moments later, he walked over and placed a ceramic soupspoon and chopsticks in front of me. He noticed my camera sitting on the countertop and turned and pointed to a handwritten sign on the wall that said NO PHOTOS. I nodded and smiled. He then softly said something to me in Japanese—I am clueless. He turned and grabbed a bottle of beer from his cooler. "Ah, yes," I nodded, and he placed the bottle in front of me. That was all the interaction I had with him until I left.

The aroma that filled the room was itself worth the visit. From the three pots he had simmering on his stove came a beef-scented steam that made my stomach growl. To say that ramen is basically broth and noodles is an insulting understatement. Preparing good ramen broth is a laborious process of simmering bones, meats, herbs, and aromatics, one that takes days to develop the depth of flavor, the richness, the color, the aroma, and the clarity—all unique to its particular chef. The noodle dough he made was slowly hand-kneaded every morning and fed through an antique noodle cutter he displayed on the side. The thickness, the firmness, and the length of the noodles all play a part in the beautiful outcome.

As he turned away from me, he picked up a large, white bowl with two hands and placed it on his work area. He took a nest of noodles from a burlap-lined tray and gently dropped them into boiling water. While they cooked, he slowly sliced a few vegetables and obscure mushrooms, and a few slices of roasted pork, placing it all in the bowl. Everything he did was calm and peaceful, almost Zen-like. On the side were about six small tins filled with assorted powders—I had no idea what they could be, but a pinch of each went into the bowl. The noodles were then added, lifted from the boiling water by a wire sieve, and followed by a large ladle of his steaming hot broth. To finish his ramen, he softly arranged a nest of finely shredded scallions and a few radish sprouts on top, picked it up with two hands, and placed it in front of me. He said nothing. For the next half hour, as I slurped each bite, I thought how fortunate I was to try this great chef's work of simplicity and absolute perfection. For a chef, eating a dish perfectly prepared sets a standard, not only for a ramen bowl, but also for food in general. It teaches us how good something can be.

One Sunday afternoon, exploring a side street in Hong Kong, I turned the corner to find a humble restaurant façade that had rows of shiny, lacquered Peking ducks hanging from hooks in the front window. The front door never stopped swinging from the crowd going in and coming out. I went inside to see a large lobby area with Chinese patrons waiting, shoulder to shoulder, for tables. I thought, *I have to eat here.*

You should always eat where there's a crowd.

After an hour, I was led to a central dining room. The room was vast and had a faint aroma of smoke. It had bright, harsh lights, no decorations, no music playing, and no ambiance whatsoever—just tables with white cloths on them and the exhilarating energy of loudly talking locals. Someone ran by my table and threw paper napkins and chopsticks at it. Then I sat there for ten minutes.

Abruptly, a man arrived and stared at me. He had no expression, stone-faced. I immediately realized he didn't speak English (funny how Americans expect everyone to speak English). Next to me was another man carving a duck at the table. I pointed to the duck and then nodded my head yes. He got the message. For the next twenty minutes, I sat there and watched a ballet of servers flying through the room. Everyone was eating just one thing: Peking duck.

My God, I couldn't wait.

At one point, a *guéridon* was wheeled to the table, displaying a few small dishes of hoisin sauce, sliced scallions, folded *crêpes*, and a large platter on which sat a perfect, gorgeous, Peking duck. The man pushing the cart did not seem like a server, but more like a cook. He was old and scrawny, with blurry green tattoos on his arms. He scattered the small dishes on my table, stood the duck upright on his tray, and with a thin-bladed knife, swiftly and masterfully carved like a surgeon until only a boney carcass was left. The duck was placed on the table and he pushed away back to the kitchen. I spied on other tables to learn what to do—smearing a crêpe with the sweet sauce and rolling up a scallion, some duck, and some brown, crispy skin into a luscious, divine bundle. It was absolute excellence. I was in heaven.

As a chef, these moments are great gifts of inspiration.

When I return home from these adventures, I am transformed. They change my awareness, and I look at the world and its inhabitants differently. I realize how little I actually know and immediately begin thinking about where the next voyage will take me.

Back in my kitchen, I always humbly attempt to re-create the dishes and the magic they conjure for my friends and my customers who have not yet made the journey. Everyone is always so captivated, especially my cooks, who have a childlike fascination about how the world eats and the exotic foods we attempt to re-create. A restaurant cook does not cook to make money. They all share an innate passion for cooking—otherwise, they would never make it through the daily drudgery and harsh conditions of a restaurant kitchen.

So, where do you find a chef? Where do you find someone to do all this? I have always been quite certain that the chef should own all or a big part of a restaurant. Chef-centric restaurants, those that are built to feature the cooking talents of an *owner*, are almost always the best.

Years ago, restaurants were often named after the guy in the kitchen, like Pierre's, or Oscar's, or Ed's Place—it was common. These days, these chef-owned places are usually the ones who get the most impressive online ratings, the ones who create institutions that last for years and spawn other cooks to open their own places. Otherwise, to lead your kitchen, you are forced to hire a chef as an employee and that is typically what you get—an employee.

Often, these young hired chefs are spit out by Napa-type restaurants and have tatted arms and wear short-sleeved chef coats that are tight around their biceps, stain free, pressed like cardboard, and they wrap American flag bandanas around their shaved heads.

These guys usually suck.

Their résumés list a dozen highly rated, pretentious restaurants where they had worked a few months and then moved on. Their goal is to ultimately open their own place. If you are opening a restaurant and have to rely on one of these idols, they will likely manage your kitchen for a while, sucking your bank account dry with an offensive salary that you willingly pay because you are desperate and you think they're going to be worth it. Soon after the hype of opening, they move on to another struggling restaurateur, who again puts faith in him or her to "save" his kitchen. I have seen it many times, and it's sad. These guys come, and they go. And what really sucks is that often, when they leave, they take at least one cook with them, the best one. Now you have to search for another transient rock star, and you end up late at night, slopped at your bar with a drink in your hand, wounded, rejected, and abandoned. "Oh God, what am I going to do now?"

You see, it is quite different when the chef owns the joint. An owner is always there. It is his home. He has sweated for years, seared his fingers and arms, cursed at servers, gone to extremes to make sure no food is ever wasted, and walked through hell to get where he is. Now he is king. He would work for free and sleep on a stainless-steel kitchen table all night if it meant the restaurant would become successful and make money.

I know because this was my life. I was always there. It was always my baby.

Thirty years ago, as a young cook bopping around kitchens, I occasionally found myself working sauté in prestigious, trend-setting restaurants whose kitchens were led by aspiring new chefs, many of whom went on to illustrious careers of acclaimed restaurants, the names of which you would certainly recognize, as well as the celebrated chefs who spawned them. One of these chefs, a hefty young woman with big, rosy cheeks, a food-genius brain, and the ability to season something perfectly, was hired by a Los Angeles company to design a menu, hire staff, and open an enormous eatery. I was brought on to work with her in this great effort as her sous chef and was thrilled to be involved with such a rising culinary star.

Working in busy restaurant kitchens, you frequently find yourself in close quarters, face next to face over a stove, or helping someone pull a pan out of an oven, or even just running around a corner. I noticed that, often, this culinary star smelled of alcohol but always put it off to some night-before drinking she may have done. Early one morning, as some of the cooks and I finished our coffee, she asked me if I wanted more. I answered, "Sure," and she took my cup and headed to the bar when the coffee machine was. I remembered I had to ask her something, and as I walked through the kitchen door to follow her, I noticed that she had just put our cups on the bar. She grabbed the coffee pot, filled mine with coffee, and then put the pot back. She then turned around, grabbed a bottle of gin from the bar, and filled her empty coffee cup halfway with gin. Yep, straight, room-temperature gin—at eight thirty in the morning.

From that moment on, as we worked through the day, I was neurotically aware that a coffee cup was *always* in her hand, and as often as I could, I'd stretch my neck to peer in the cup. It was never coffee. She drank gin out of her cup the entire day, which explained why, by evening service, she was always so silly and giggly, and why she always had those big, rosy cheeks. As weeks passed, her lack of competence became more and more apparent to both me and the proprietors of the business—schedules weren't done, purchasing was either grossly overestimated or we were out of menu items, and all the other typical duties of an executive chef were neglected.

One day, she was asked by a managing partner to add a few cheeses for sale in a display case along with all the sandwiches and salads that we made every morning. Later that afternoon, as she teetered in her office chair, she got on the phone with a vendor and I eavesdropped as she began to order cheese—a lot of cheese. As she browsed through a catalogue, I could hear her say, ". . . and I'll take ten Stilton wheels, and a couple of dozens of Camemberts, and six wheels of Gruyere, and eight Gouda, and three Reggio Parmesan wheels, oh yes, and I love Asiago, give me twenty, and . . ." For fifteen minutes, she ordered cheeses, high-end, expensive, imported cheeses, sometimes pausing a moment forgetting a thought, then snapping back to order more. It became apparent to me that she was not in reality, but instead, in some illusory place with no regard to what she was doing. It was sad to see this, what alcohol had done to the life of this talented woman with such great potential.

The next morning when I arrived, I opened the door of the large, walk-in refrigerator to a wall of cheese, so much cheese that you could not squeeze by to get in. I ran to see the invoice that the delivery driver had left to see what happened. The invoice totaled almost ten thousand dollars' worth of cheese—enough for a year, or more. Cheese that was supposed to fill a three-foot space in a display case. When the chef arrived around noon, she went into the office behind a closed door with one of the owners. I did not see her for the rest of the day. Later, the owner asked me to try to return the cheeses. A day later, the managing partners called me and another sous chef to the office and told us that the superstar chef—this highly paid, highly anticipated culinary virtuoso—had to return back east and would not be with us anymore. We were asked to take over the operation and try to fix the unimaginable mess. Within two weeks, cooks and servers started to leave because pay checks bounced, and vendors wouldn't deliver anything unless they were paid in cash. I stayed on another couple of weeks, without pay, until one final morning when I was told the doors were closing. This enormous investment of money and effort was lost.

You don't always get what you pay for when you hire a chef—time tells the truth.

─────────────

I am now set to staff all the departments—to handpick the motley group of soldiers who will execute my plan. As I interview the candidates, the servers, the hosts, the cooks, the bus staff, and as they sit across from me touting their virtues, a voice keeps whispering in my ear, "You're only as good as those who work for you—do I really want this guy here?" I know that some people I hire will leave in a week; others just aren't right, and I will painfully let them go. Others will become alcoholics, or perhaps an old drug dependence will resurface. Some will remain friends for years and I'll become *padrino* to their firstborn son, others I'll visit in the hospital, others will die in a car accident or from an overdose or from cancer or commit suicide. It has all happened. During the late 1980s, when AIDS was taking the lives of so many, it seemed every week I knew someone who died, sometimes employees, or their friends, and many times customers. Employees of a restaurant are often runaways and loners, people who left their hometowns to build a life somewhere else. The bonds they make with each other under the stresses of service are strong and often lasting.

So, I sit there and deliberate whether I should hire a server who has a cool personality but wears a metal nose ring, or another who looks like a fitness cover model with a sparkling smile but has not waited tables since college—servers come in all shapes and sizes. The process is nerve-racking since I know my choices can make or break me.

But for these people, it is just a job. They just have to pay rent.

Serving tables is thankless work, but being a server, one learns much about human nature, how people behave, and how to react to on-the-spot crises and volatile situations. Servers learn to accept criticism and develop the skills to salvage a table gone south and rescue a sinking ship. There is an empathy and patience that only comes from being on the other side, from standing at a table with a smile on their face in the aggressive throes of the public. Everyone should have to wait tables for some period of time.

Over the years, I have employed thousands of these drifters. Sometimes, they are with me for decades. Other times, after a week or two, they walk off the floor in the middle of a busy night overloaded by the stress that accompanies the job. Many have arrived drunk, trying to focus their eyes as they sway back and forth at a computer terminal, others are drenched in sweat, high on some drug. I have found servers half naked playing around in the storeroom, and then there was Juan, one of the best I ever had—handsome, friendly, able to serve half the dining room himself—who, at the end of weekend shifts, took his gym bag into the men's room and, half an hour later, emerged as Juanita, full makeup, wig, dress, and heels, ready to hit the town for a drink after work. It's a cavalcade of characters.

What I know about servers is that most of them, if not all, are waiting tables because they cannot make money doing something else. In Los Angeles, every server I ever had was connected in some way to the movie industry. Most were bright, beautiful, budding actors—all magnetism and personality. At tableside, this is the perfect storm. They are on stage, performers that they are, and can charm just about anyone into ordering the most decadent desert. They are good, so very good, when they want to be.

Moments later, I hear one boasting too loud at the bus station or in the kitchen about an upcoming audition or how close he was to getting his SAG card. I think, *Would you just focus on your tables while you're here? I don't give a shit about your SAG card.* Then I hear another complain that her section is being seated unfairly, that the host was favoring someone else. Then another forgets someone's entrée and the table is pissed and now wants to see a manager. And then another says he refuses to wait on table 8 because his ex is sitting there. Then another drops a bottle of balsamic vinegar, it shatters on the dining room carpet, and she is now hysterically crying. And on and on it goes. I breathe to myself, smile, and one by one, put out the fires. A good manager does this throughout service. It is their job to control the chaos and the drama. It never ends.

You have to keep reaching up into the air as these people float away and pull them back to Earth.

This in mind, I shuffle through the résumés, often with an attached 8x10 glossy headshot of the applicant, the one they use for auditions, and handpick the front-of-the-house staff, the new face of my business, the personality of the dining room. I schedule the first of many pre-opening meetings. They all show up, two come a half hour early, most arrive on time, and a couple are five minutes late and sweaty. I think, *Why the hell are you late? What could possibly cause you to be late on your first day? It's the most important thing you've got going on.*

But I say nothing.

I ask them to gather in the dining room. Where they sit in the room speaks volumes. Some group together in the center chatting with each other, and others sit self-importantly alone. And so begins the formation of boundaries that employees set that will soon drive me insane.

When I ask everyone to introduce themselves, the first says, "Adam." And that's it.

The next says, "Hi everyone I'm Heather and I'm really glad that I'm here and I've been a waitress my whole life and I live in the valley but I'm originally from Tucson where my parents used to own a diner but when I was twelve we moved to Costa Mesa because my dad whose brother lived in Tarzana decided to . . ."

This goes on five minutes.

It now becomes clear that Heather is a talker. Within a week or so, I find myself walking around the far side of the dining room just to avoid her.

But I must fight the battle with the soldiers I have.

As I hand out menus and wine lists to begin their education, I start with my own story. This is key since my narrative, the stories I tell, and the words and phrases I use, are the ones that linger in their heads and are those they use when speaking with customers. Good servers say what you tell them to say.

This process is generally repeated for the buss staff, though they do not have headshots. They just really want to work, and as much as possible. And they always have a cousin who is looking for work, as well. They are right in par with the dishwashers as the hardest working people in a restaurant and are the first to arrive and the last to leave, patiently waiting for their tips every night. They set the dining room, polish everything, spend their evening running in every direction as servers bark at them, carry heavy tubs of dirty plates back to the kitchen, and are the ones who get to clean up a bachelorette's barf from the ladies' room floor, the one who drank three Mai Tais in ten minutes.

Blessed are the hosts, the face of the restaurant, those proverbial punching bags standing at the front desk, taking good and bad shots all night long. They must smile through madness, regardless of what's going on in their heads, because no one wants to see a pissed off Mickey Mouse at Disneyland. When customers step through the door, they are often coming from a frazzled reality, stressed from driving or finding parking or hurrying to make the reservation, and it is that energy that they bring into the restaurant and to the face of the host. They announce their name with a confrontational brashness, and they stare with fixed eyes as the host searches the book, running through the reservations, always hoping silently that the name is there—a moment later, one might hear, "Is there a problem?" If the name is *not* there, and a table is available, a good host will likely just pretend the reservation exists, "Oh, there it is," and seat the party, all the while maintaining a calm customer service protocol, pretty smiles and cheeriness, just part of the job description. Whether or not the customer actually made the reservation is of little consequence; since they *believe* they made it, it better be there. And for the record, slipping the host some cash *always* gets you preferred status and what you want—it's obvious when a host pulls a party ahead of the crowd and seats them out of order. Someone has paid for first class.

Most customers are humble and are quite excited to be seated and subsequently enjoy time with their friends at their table. But there are most certainly a privileged few who come in like they own the joint, boldly acknowledging the staff by name, seemingly knowing everyone, walking around, digging the vibe, noticing the crowd, and will most definitely require a full tour of all possible tables they could have. Many will only sit at a specific table, something that is made quite clear when they make the reservation, and even if the table next to it, exactly like it, just four feet to one side, is available, it is unacceptable.

It's not quite as simple as one might think to guarantee a specific table for a guest. A busy restaurant's goal is to maximize its seating, and the timing of tables coming and going is a learned skill that a seasoned host masters—they understand that older couples generally eat quickly and leave, but four women on a Saturday, and you can kiss the table goodbye for the night. A table of millennials will often sit wordlessly for a half hour after they paid the check, lost in their cell phones. All the while you have some guy in your face because he was promised *that* table. Other times, a birthday party of eight people may arrive with gifts that must be opened one at a time, eating up an extra hour at the table, or another table may pull out a laptop to conduct a business meeting after dinner, or maybe some guy decides at the last minute, just when you think they're going to get up, to have a cup of coffee before he drives home, another half hour. None of this is ever disclosed when the reservation is made, nor can it be predicted, and it layers a smiling host's job of seating a busy restaurant with obstacles, challenges, surprises, and stress—it is truly the labor of saints.

Over the next couple of months, my well-picked opening team will likely fade away. For some reason, the opening staff always tends to move on. There may be a few that stay around for years and even become lifelong friends, but for the most part, they quickly vanish into the night. Once the restaurant runs for a while and I can get a better sense on what kind of *personality* fits, the success rate greatly improves. Until then, I hire and train then repeat. It is what I have to do.

———————————

Cooks, on the other hand, come from another galaxy. In Southern California, these soldiers are Latinos. Period. You might find a couple of white guys spattered here and there, and for the most part, they usually suck. The A-team comes from Mexico, with a touch of Guatemala and Salvador in the mix, and the language on the line and throughout the kitchen is most definitely Spanish.

I was raised with Italian speakers, so when I arrived at my first SoCal cooking gig, the Spanish came easily to me. Over the years, I have gotten pretty good—good enough to understand the yelling during service, and good enough to know when someone talks shit about me. That part you learn fast.

Being able to converse also helps you sympathize with the struggles these immigrants have, like when their car is stolen, or they are back in rent, or they need a loan because their grandmother died the night before in Mexico and they have to send money. Life is not easy for them, but they are indeed a happy lot. Money for the family is more important than time off, and they often flip eggs in the morning at one restaurant, then drive to another to cook dinner six nights a week. One paycheck barely makes it to the next. Plus, I have never met one who did not regularly wire money back to Mexico for their mom or some aunt. And for the record, female line cooks are among the sweetest, kindness people you'll ever meet. They are caring, hardworking, and reliable— but—during high pressure dinner service, it's a Jekyll and Hyde scenario—they turn into monsters ready to rip your throat apart if you even get near their stations or God forbid, ask them if what they're cooking is ready. Even the male line cooks know to leave them be.

When I hire a cook, I ask two questions: Where were you working before? And how long were you there? Their answer does not really matter since most of it is probably bullshit. I believe little a cook tells me during an interview and usually just look for burns on their arms or how beat up their shoes are to judge their merit. It is only when he or she grabs a knife and dices an onion in fifteen seconds that I know I have made the right call.

Dishwashers, those transient souls who slog through the night in the back corridors of the kitchen, scrubbing pots and pans with chaffed hands, loading commercial dishwashing machines, enduring heat and humidity, dripping with sweat, are among the hardest working people anywhere. They spend their shifts lifting heavy racks of plates and glassware, strapped with lifting belts around their waists, and wear wet clothing that's dotted from splattered bleach. I always try to remember that they are children of God, not slaves, since that's how they are often treated. No matter what happens—someone spills a five-gallon bucket of tomato sauce, the floor drain clogs up, a greasy oven needs to be cleaned, or a toilet overflows—get the dishwasher. Despite the papers and IDs they produce when hired, these migrants always seem as though they just ran across the border, clad in dusty jeans and a tired shirt they wore a week ago on the *ranchero*. They move around with a guarded look in their eyes as they try to make sense of this strange new world. I learned many years ago that a most curious quality shared by all dishwashers is a propensity to lie. You never get the truth, even if it doesn't really matter. Why they really miss a shift is certainly not what they tell you—they'll say their ride didn't show and their phone was dead, but another cook later tells me the guy was drinking tequila until five. Then I find myself bribing someone else with a handful of twenty-dollar bills to work his shitty shift, praying the dishwasher shows up tomorrow. If he doesn't, it's likely I'll never see him again—they always just vanish into the night.

So, the whole crew, the men and women in my culinary entourage, come together. If I treat them with respect, comradery, and really care about their lives as friends do, I will likely be blessed with a team who becomes family and works with me for many years. From a chef's perspective, this is heaven. Most of what I do in the kitchen is teach cooks how to cook—it's an ongoing process that is made much easier when they stick around. If a restaurant's kitchen has much turnover, it's the chef's fault.

Dad used to say that the fish stinks from the head.

It's often the case that when I do find a respectable line cook—one that has a natural ability to make good food, who knows how hot an oiled skillet should be before they lay in a fish, or how to appropriately salt and pepper a lamb chop, including the bone—it is not uncommon that they have a brother, or sister, or husband, or wife, who are good cooks, as well. It tends to run in the family and many times I've built my staff with relatives—the innate talents are there, maybe genetic, or maybe they come from a food-family, as I do, and they are apt to help and take care of each other. My best cooks have come to me this way. Sometimes I tolerate reckless behavior, like pounding a couple beers before, or even during, their shift, just because they are so good. Other times, I keep around not-so-good cooks simply because they are devoted and I like them so much, like a salad lady I once had. We used to call her "the squeezer." To make a salad, she'd put the greens in a bowl, drizzle them with dressing, and go down on the salad with her hand, literally punching and squeezing the lettuces, like she was washing her clothes in a river. For years, I tried to correct her. I'd show her how to gently toss the leaves, lifting them lightly and tenderly. She'd say, "Oh, okay," and then squeeze again. I would just cringe and walk away.

If employees feel appreciated, they will do more than what's expected.

The diligence of these soldiers is remarkable. There have been Saturday nights when the exhaust has failed, and my cooks endure a hot, smoky kitchen to finish the last tickets on the line. There have been broken ovens and fryers, power failures, and nights when half the kitchen calls in sick, leaving the task of cooking to just a few healthy people; or when a cook's wife goes into labor at 6:00 p.m. on a Saturday and he runs out the door, leaving the kitchen in a frenzy for the next four hours. And then in Palm Springs, there are those balmy evenings when the outside temperature is 110 degrees and the guys on the line have towels wrapped around their heads to absorb the sweat. Or when the ticket printers are down, and everyone is chaotically screaming food orders back and forth in Spanish.

I could go on forever with horror stories from the kitchen. And while all that hysteria is unfolding, on the other side of those swinging doors sits a dining room of people sipping martinis and chatting away. But, let me tell you, when my cooks are in the zone, it is a feeling I cannot describe. On busy nights, standing on the side, watching a talented group of twelve or so hard-working Latinos pass hot plates back and forth, trying their very best to make each one perfect, working in difficult conditions, laughing and pushing through, has made me literally tear up. When it works, when the cooking machine is humming, it is a beautiful spectacle of talent, devotion, and respect.

———————

Uniforms have now been passed out. W-2s are completed. Opening night's date has been set. The management team schedules staff meetings and begins training.

Menus are meticulously explained down to specific ingredients and most of the servers start closing their eyes after the first half hour. Now come the wine lists, computerized order-taking systems, table sections, bussing procedures, reservation systems, and on and on. It all has to be painstakingly instructed because despite what any of the front-of-the-house staff tells you and how much experience they say they have, they really don't know what they're doing.

I am now days away from opening. The phone lines are ringing, my cell is ringing, and different vendors appear every five minutes and just stand there waiting until I have time to listen to their pitches. Stacked everywhere are pallets of china and glassware, cases of wine and liquor, and boxes of silverware that have to be put away. The contractor is still completing final touches and there is an odd mix of construction people and service staff running around.

I now must begin the onerous task of, as chefs say, *bringing up the kitchen*. Thousands of ingredients have to be ordered, received, and organized. It is like stocking a grocery store, and as things arrive, wheeled in on dollies from delivery trucks, no one has any idea where anything belongs. It is just overwhelming. Deliveries are often missing items, or the avocados are hard as rocks, or the lettuces are wet and wilted from yesterday's rain; they have to be sent back and reordered. I ordered a special Japanese noodle for the ramen, but instead they sent some frozen Chinese stuff.

Cooks show up and try to learn a menu they have never seen before. They aimlessly run around and wonder which station makes what and how it is prepared. I am talking out of both sides of my mouth, trying to keep calm and trying to give everyone direction, but my fucking phone keeps ringing. Now the oven won't light. I have to find the plumber to check the gas connection. There is no time to make a schedule for the next day, and I don't even know anyone's name yet—instead, I point. "Hey, you come tomorrow at nine and you come at three."

This hell lasts about a week.

On the eve of opening day, usually with a partner and maybe a manager, I sit at the bar late at night with a bottle of Cabernet. I quietly gaze around and sigh at my great feat of accomplishment. I feel proud, like the father of a newborn. I see the menus are set out at the host stand and are ready to go, the oil and vinegar cruets are filled, though I am forced to use some shitty breadbaskets because I was told at the last minute that the ones I ordered were out of stock. The place is set for dinner and sparkles like the main dining hall of the *Queen Mary* on her maiden voyage.

None of us really talk since our brains and our bodies are exhausted. It is quiet, and I can faintly hear the kitchen refrigeration humming. The place smells oddly like a combination of food and fresh paint, and my hands, for the first time in years, smell like fish from the filleting I did earlier. My journey of more than a year has brought me to this moment. It is midnight and I realize that this is my new normal—late nights and exhaustion, but I try to encourage myself that it will get better, easier, and will morph into an unruffled routine.

Time to head home. Lights out. My poor dog hasn't peed all day.

HORRORS

*"The next noise to echo through the room was
one I was quite sure I recognized.
It was the unmistakable sound of the shit hitting the fan."*

NICOLE PEELER

When I attended culinary school, a French chef started class one morning with the tale of an opening night at a grand hotel in Switzerland where he worked many years ago. They chose New Year's Eve to open and were inundated with hundreds of black-tie VIPs in the main ballroom. He told of how the kitchen was buried with orders. In those days, there were no fancy computer ticket printers—instead, the chef would get the order from a server and scream it out to the busy line cooks. At the height of the evening's chaos, an over-weight, tough old cook, sweating like a horse from the heat of his grill, red-faced and panting, fell to the floor holding his chest and died. For just a few seconds, the kitchen stopped and turned their heads. The chef ran behind the cooking line, grabbed the old cook by his feet, dragged him down the aisle to the walk-in refrigerator, opened the door, and pulled the poor chap inside. And there he lay "on ice" for hours until service was over.

The show must go on.

No one has ever died during any of my opening nights, though I did work at one place years ago where the owner, three hours into his first night of service, had to literally be carried out on a stretcher by paramedics. These nights are absolutely, most definitely, always horror stories from hell, and no amount of planning or know-how prepares you for the shit that goes down.

Why this undeniable reality occurs is twofold: First, for some really screwed up reason, it is crucial for cer-tain people to try your place *the very first night*, and second, the stark reality that your staff is new, inex-perienced, and generally clueless. This volatile combi-nation of forces swirls together and explodes like hot soup in a covered blender. At the end of the night, you are left ravaged, and your new restaurant ends up look-ing like a Cat 5 blew through.

Many years ago, I get the not-so-brilliant idea to do

a pre-opening dinner at a Los Angeles restaurant and invite the trades who built the place, and their families, to a "dress rehearsal." Plumbers, electricians, contactors, accountants, PR people, and friends of the newly hired staff were asked to make reservations and attend this hosted night. They could order anything from the menu to try—all they had to pay for was alcohol.

Sounds fair, right? Like a nice thing to do, right?

Everyone arrives at the same time, even though reservations had been carefully spaced out. The first ticket prints up in the kitchen—it is a table of four. They order four appetizers, four salads, four *steak* entrées (the most expensive choice on the menu), and they want to try two other entrées, the scallops and the salmon.

When I see the ticket, I say to the server, "What the hell is this? It's four people. This night is so people can *try* something we make, not gorge up for the winter. Go tell them to reorder."

The server nervously goes back, retakes the order but does not know how to adjust the availability in the computer. This time they want one steak, one sea bass, two salmon, two appetizers, and one salad. So, the server decides to ring an entirely *new* ticket into the computer and leave the old one still in there. The computer system had been preset with a specific count of how many of each item was available for the night and now, after the very first ticket, the count is off.

This occurs within the first five minutes of opening. An hour later, the system warns that we are out of steaks, though we actually have more, so confused servers reenter other items randomly, getting errors that they are unavailable, screw up the counts again, and retake orders, reenter, etc. It gets so bad that I just start yelling out what we have before they go to the table. I would tell them we have one salmon left and by the time they put the order in the system, another server takes it. No one gets what they order—it's a fucking mess.

These sophisticated order-entry systems are a big part of opening night issues. They are programed with all your stuff by some tech somewhere, and despite what you tell him, items are entered in the wrong categories, missing, or coded to print to the wrong printers.

That night, for example, it turns out that a *bar printer* had been printing some of the *food* items by mistake. When I discover the issue, I tell the bartender to run these tickets to the kitchen if he gets a food item. But as the night progresses, this guy is so buried making drinks, he forgets half of the tickets—so a table is often shorted an item since the kitchen never gets the ticket. All you see are panic-stricken servers chaotically running around trying to figure out what is happening.

At one point, a server turns to me and blurts, "Table 18 says that no one told them that alcohol wasn't included, so they don't want to pay for it."

I say to her, "No, they were clearly told when they were invited that *food* was complimentary. Who are they?"

"I don't know," she says.

"Well, what did they order?"

She mumbles, "Ah, two bottles of Pine Ridge Cabernet." ($90 a bottle.)

"Huh?! Well, they have to fucking pay for them. Just put the check back on the table and say, 'Sorry, folks, only food was complimentary tonight.'"

"But . . ."

"Go!"

I know what's going to happen. They'll want to see me. People always love to ask to see a manager. What they do not realize is that the server is just telling them what *they were told to say by the manager.* They want to try to convince me they are right and negotiate a deal.

Well, sure enough, she comes back to me and says, "They want to talk to a manager."

Now, I am up to my ass in crises at this point and everything is going wrong. Cooks are lost. Food looks like garbage. Servers don't even know what items we're still serving. People have waited an hour for dinner, and now I have to stop and go talk with some punks who don't want to pay for the wine they drank.

So, I stop, take a breath, and walk over to the table.

"Hi. What's going on?"

A thirty-year-old blond girl wearing enough perfume to make my eyes water says, "Ah, yes, we got the bill, and our wine was on it. We were told that everything was complimentary tonight."

"Who told you that?"

"My roommate."

"Who's your roommate?"

"Amanda. She's one of your servers here," she says.

I grin, pause, and say, "Well, she's wrong. I'll send Amanda over to explain." And I walk away.

I find Amanda, who is a frazzled mess because she is so behind with orders. As she runs by, she stops and turns to me—it's as though she has just seen the face of the devil. She knows what I'm going to say.

"Amanda, go to table 18. Your roommate is there. She says she was never told about the no-free-alcohol rule tonight. Tell her that either she pays for it, or you do."

That was it. Done with that. One fire put out.

When I get back to the kitchen, the situation is worse. Servers are standing like hungry beggars in a food line trying to get something for their tables to eat. I keep handing them plates and yell, "Just take it to the table! That's all we have!"

A moment later, a server comes hurling into the kitchen and blurts out, "Chef, chef, I have a vegan at the table. What do we have for a vegan?"

For the record, the only chef who likes to cook for

vegans is a vegan chef.

When a server tells the kitchen in a busy restaurant that they have a vegan, the chef and cooks all mumble *fuck* under their breath.

Like a wiseass, I yell, "I have vegetables!"

The server runs back to the dining room, returns in a minute, and approaches me with caution—he is well aware of my wrath and my surging blood pressure.

"She wants to know what kind," he bumbles nervously.

"Huh?!"

"What kind . . . she wants to know what you have."

"Broccoli. We have broccoli. That's it!"

And off he went. A half hour later, a ticket comes out of the printer with three entrées from the menu and one plate of broccoli. Remember, the purpose of this night was to try the menu, to experience our cuisine. She ate broccoli.

By the end of the night, the staff is trashed. My poor servers are beat up by invited guests who complained that their free food took too long. The line cooks look like soccer players defeated in the finals, walking slowly as they clean up, silent and conquered. Amanda never mentions what happened with table 18, and I don't really care. We strategize to fix what had gone wrong because tomorrow night, it gets real—the curtain goes up and the paying public comes filing in.

Sadly, the first few nights are when amateur critics often come out. It is when they call friends the next day and say either, "Oh God, I went to the best new restaurant last night," or they say, "I went to this new place last night and God, was it horrible." They impulsively rate what you worked for years to achieve without compassion and understanding for just how difficult it all can be.

The first night always seems to be judgment day.

After two years of brutal construction, I open my Palm Springs restaurant and suffer a similar, inevitable fate. The first two nights are beasts. Highly anticipated, this dazzling, brand new restaurant, touting big expectations in a town lacking competition, is just overcome with hundreds and hundreds of people on both nights. People clamor at the front desk, waiting for a table. Some walk out, roll their eyes, and blurt, "Good luck, man," and others say, "What a beautiful place. We're so glad you're here!" As always, these nights are plagued by the top two evils— inexperienced staff and technical problems.

Try as they might, an opening staff, both kitchen and front-of-the-house, crashes and burns under pressure. Everything is easy when you are proficient and have been doing it for a while. The server knows how many shrimp come on an appetizer—no need to stop, run back to the kitchen, find the chef, and then return to the table with the answer. And a cook's muscle memory automatically tosses a pinch of oregano in the pasta and does not pause to refer to a recipe card's ingredient list. A seasoned restaurant purrs efficiently—and during the first couple weeks, nothing about a new restaurant is efficient.

The public expects you to be spot-on the first day and loves to let you know when you are not.

By the third night, things are improving. The host stand is still jammed at 7:00 p.m., but the staff begins to flow and develop a choreography—servers hurry around with direction and intent, not quite as chaotic and flustered as they were the first two nights, and though the kitchen is still backed up, the food is looking better and is finally being served hot. It is a blustery Friday night, and a desert storm is predicted to come in. By eight, a torrential downpour hits. Over the sound of the kitchen exhaust, I can hear the rain pounding on the roof. At one point, I notice water trickling down the walls of the kitchen. Within a minute, these trickles turn into streams. Then water starts gushing through the ceiling as though all the pipes have pulled apart. It is literally raining in the kitchen—everywhere—to the point that cooks are wiping their heads with towels.

What the fuck is going on!?

My partner grabs a construction ladder lying outside, goes up to the roof, and runs back to the kitchen, screaming, "The fucking electricians never sealed the holes they drilled in the roof. That's where the water's coming from!"

There are probably twenty (one-inch) holes draining the flooded roof into the kitchen.

By now, the kitchen rainfall had created an inch of water on the entire floor and everyone's shoes are soaked through. The servers are tracking water into the dining room and people are slipping and falling everywhere. We are throwing away plates of food because they are filled with roof water, and the fryers are popping from water drizzling into the hot oil. My partner jumps in his car and runs home to get a pump. When he returns, there's so much water in the kitchen, it's flowing out the back door like a water main had broken — a literal flood everywhere. We set up the pump, but it's basically useless. Big chunks of saturated drywall and insulation are falling down from the ceiling and plopping everywhere. My cooks and I are completely soaked, as though we had fallen into a swimming pool, and there are two hundred people in the dining room getting pissed and restless as they wait for dinner.

We let the pump run all night. When we get there the next morning at seven, my new, gleaming kitchen is trashed. The ceiling tiles and drywall had continued to fall through the night and had actually cooked onto the hot stovetops. An hour later, as we cleaned, the produce company arrives with my delivery. I do not even know where to stack it since everything is still wet, but I need it because fuck, it's Saturday — we have a full house of reservations.

And again, as is always the case, the show must go on.

Over the next week, the kitchen and the roof are repaired, but for many years later, the scars from the patched drywall remained in clear view—as did my sordid memories from the night it rained in the kitchen.

The tales of what has transpired from years in the restaurant business are more unbelievable than one could imagine. Horrors strike at you like lightning bolts from nowhere—you cannot plan on the air conditioner burning up and blowing oily smoke into a packed dining room when it is 100 degrees outside, or the internet dying on Saturday night with hundreds of people in the house, leaving you with no music, no reservation system, no phone, and no credit card authorizations.

By the way, in a cruel twist of fate, these disasters have an uncanny way of befalling on a Saturday, usually around 6:00 p.m. when you just get going. This is the bewitching hour when the power fails, or a cook finds out his grandmother just died and he has to leave, or a toilet in the ladies' room bubbles up and a surge of stinking sewage flows out from under the door and into the lobby. Some nights I feel like an amateur boxer mismatched with a champion who just keeps punching me, one after the next.

How many times I've looked up and said, "What the fuck else could go wrong?"

On my list of the topmost horrifying restaurant nightmares, I undoubtedly include those times when the computerized order entry system crashes. Everything is done by way of this system—servers enter orders, authorize credit cards, and keep track of their tables, and the kitchen uses printed tickets so the cooks know what to cook and the expeditor, the guy who puts a table's food all together, can figure out what goes with what. When this system goes down, everything stops. It is cardiac arrest. We are on life support.

I have suffered through more than my share of evenings trying to decipher servers' handwritten notes, yelling to cooks what to make, and trying to get customers their food—it's just a mess, and it always happens when you have a packed house. The manager frantically runs in circles trying to show servers how to use the old handheld credit card imprint device with a cell phone pressed to his ear, on hold with the system's customer service department. And wouldn't you know it, miraculously, it all comes back online just minutes before the restaurant closes, after the night from hell has taken its toll.

Tragically, as I work though my list, in no particular order of stomach-churning stress, is traumatic refrigeration failure. Restaurants typically have dozens of units, as well as large, walk-in refrigeration and freezer rooms, all of which are usually packed full of expensive food. This equipment functions under demanding conditions, doors opened and slammed closed every minute, hinges and gaskets strained, and compressors that run incessantly in a hot environment. Plus, when they die, it's often a slow death—just a little refrigeration gas hissing out of a pin hole in a copper tube. No one really notices until it's too late, when a cook tells me the shrimp are warm, or a busser says the milk is curdled. At that point, there is really nothing to do other than toss it all away and call the refrigeration repair company.

These companies, like most businesses, operate from 9 to 5, and not on weekends. But as we are well aware, everything in a restaurant breaks during the night or on the weekend. All restauranteurs know this. So, I am left despairingly paging some on-call tech who not only does not know what he's doing, but reminds me that his rate is double for overtime, then predictably tells me that he can't fix it because he needs a part that has to be ordered and it will not be in until next week. That's how it goes. It's always the same. As shitty as that might sound, if it's just a small kitchen refrigerator, it is really no more than a frustrating inconvenience for the cooks who must now work on top of one another and share a different unit.

Here is where it gets real.

Half asleep, I arrive at the kitchen early Sunday morning and my Latina prep lady informs me that the large walk-in *freezer* is not working. I open the door, go inside, and it's room temperature.

Fuck.

The fan is blowing warm air and everything I squeeze is soft and wet. Immediately, I call the refrigeration company, whose voicemail says to page an on-call technician, which I do. Knowing my chances of someone showing up within a reasonable amount of time are basically zero, I gather everyone I can find to begin the arduous task of trying to salvage what I can. For the next hour, I pour containers of melted gelato down the drain, relocate as much as I can to other freezers, and hope for the best. The technician arrives at four in afternoon, and I can tell right off that he has no idea what he is doing. He says he is the "residential" guy, but he can have the commercial guy there first thing Monday morning. I roll my eyes and say fine—I just want him to leave. Dozens of phone calls later, the freezer finally ends up working again the following Wednesday.

In a busy place, something is always malfunctioning, whether it is a refrigerator, dishwasher, hot water tank, fryer, mixer, or pizza oven. When these things go down, often the business goes down, as well. I have learned to seriously kiss the asses of these busy repairmen to be rescued, and the wisdom of my years has taught me to always keep them in good standing, paid on time, and treated with humble respect, because I know that whether they show up or not can make or break an evening. I also learned that it helps to always toss the guy a pizza on his way out. Money in the bank.

Hands down, at the top of the list of nightmares, nothing is conceivably worse than having a full restaurant—servers running, music playing, the kitchen humming along—and after two quick flashes of the lights, you are hit with a total power failure. The building goes dead. Blackout. The first words out of my mouth are, "Oh God, please let them come back on." I stand there, motionless for a moment. But they do not.

Emergency lights switch on and cast ominous shadows over the dining room. The first thing I hear is some drunk bellow at the bar, "Guess they should have paid their bill."

There's always one in the crowd.

I immediately head outside to see if the neighbors have power. Thank God, they *do not*. That means it's not our fault; it's the power company. My managers run to me for guidance, and I tell them to start begging customers to pay their bills with cash (which no one ever has) or try to manually process their credit card. Some people actually go to an ATM and return with cash, but by the end of the night, if the lights do not come back on, most tabs are not paid, and people just leave. It has happened to me more times than I care to remember.

As I push through the door to the kitchen, I walk into a thick, dark cloud of smoke, because there is no functioning ventilation system. The room has one emergency light that's illuminating all the smoke, but it's a total whiteout—I can't see anything. The cooks are smart enough to immediately shut down the gas stoves, but the hot grill, covered with steaks, chops, and dripping fat, continues to billow smoke. We open the back door of the kitchen, but it really doesn't help. In the smoke, the diligent cooks persevere for a minute or two to finish what they had cooking then they all head outside to get some air. My manager comes up to me and tells me the power company says the whole block is down and they're not sure how long the power will be out.

Now comes the most difficult part.

The unknown.

Will the power return in five minutes or will it be off for two days? These disasters unfold in a variety of ways. Sometimes an hour later, when a few customers may still be there, the lights return. Other times, it could be a day or more and I am forced to go through the whole loss-of-refrigeration-scenario I referred to earlier, packing refrigerators with ice and hoping for the best.

Regardless, these episodes just suck. Not only do I lose money from unpaid tabs and wasted food, but servers do not get tips, cooks spend the rest of their night in a smoky kitchen putting things away by the light of a phone, and massive piles of dirty dishes with dried-on food will sit to be scraped cleaned when power finally returns.

Passion and resilience get you through the days.

In beautiful Southern California, where skies are always clear, people love having dinner al fresco. That in mind, many restaurants, including all I have ever owned, are designed with open-air patios of premium tables that are often reserved well ahead of time. Since weather forecasts are usually only useful a week or so in advance, a patio can be fully reserved right in time for a storm to hit. The conditions for this disastrous scenario have come together way too many times.

It has struck on Valentine's Day, on Thanksgiving, on New Year's Eve, and on many Saturday nights—a packed house, both inside the dining room and on the patio, and a 30 percent chance of rain looming in the distance. As the evening proceeds, you can always find me off to the side with the weather forecast pulled up on my cell phone, refreshing the app every minute in hopes of a new result, that perhaps the storm has changed direction and the skies are clearing.

But you know what happens.

Though I have endured such catastrophes many times, one night in particular stands out.

It is Saturday, of course, in high season, and the house is packed. I have customers waiting for tables at the host stand, the bar is lined two deep, and every seat is taken inside the dining room and a hundred more guests are seated on the patio. The energy is high, and people are having fun. The forecast for rain is only 20 percent, good odds, and the skies are clear with thick, spotty clouds.

At one moment, someone touches my shoulder from the back. I turn around at see my busgirl standing there literally drenched. Her hair is sopping wet. She says to me in broken English, "It's raining bad." As my eyes look over her to the patio door, I see a rush of people come running inside, many with their dinner plates in hand, rustling to the front host stand. Everyone is soaked. I push through the crowd and out to the patio and walk into a desert downpour, the kind that flash floods the streets in a minute. My staff is wildly splashing though the rain trying to help guests.

Back inside, people are clamoring for a place to stand. Four people are sitting on the floor against a wall with their dinner plates in their laps. People are yelling at me, demanding an inside table. Many others just run out the door and no one pays for anything. An elderly woman looking like a wet cat comes up to me and holds her dinner plate in front of her. Her entrée is literally floating in rainwater. She softly says, "I can't eat this now." I just look at her, take the plate, and apologize, "I'm so sorry." She turns and walks away.

Sometimes there's nothing you can say to make a situation better.

At the end of the ordeal, my staff and I sit together around the bar for a drink. Everyone is there. It is quiet and calm, and the skies are clear. Our clothes are still soaked through and splashed with mud from planters that spilled over and we are all worn out from stress. It's another night to remember, another horror story for the books. As I look around at my tattered crew, I think about the nature of restaurant workers, how in crisis they unite and form a brotherhood. They are always the first to help a stranger and are the last to jump off a sinking ship.

I have no doubt whatsoever that if everyone at some point in their lives had worked in a restaurant, the world would be a better place.

But most often, when a restaurant crashes, there's really no specific catastrophic event to blame. It's not a storm, nor a power failure; it is often something one might think insignificant, or maybe just how the planets aligned that night, but it sets off a chain reaction that creates a bumper-to-bumper food jam in the kitchen and service comes to a grinding stop. Just one cook having to leave because his kid needs to go to the emergency room makes the difference between a successful Saturday night and an evening of chaos.

At the helm of a restaurant kitchen is the expeditor, the alpha dog, the dude who pulls plates from five or so cooking stations, and based on a table's ticket, puts them all together so everything is presented to your table in unison. He's also the only one with whom the servers may speak; servers know never to talk to cooks directly—it is ubiquitously forbidden—and if they do, cooks know to ignore them or to bark out a string of Latin obscenities and accompanying hand gestures. Expediting was always my job, since I could visually inspect each plate before it departs the kitchen, and if I needed something fast from a stressed-out cook, they did it without giving me shit.

You know, chefs ideally want to make perfect food. We want every plate to express what we've taken years to learn, using only the finest seasonal ingredients, everything placed perfectly on the plate, mouthwateringly beautiful. In this fantasy world, we'd love to prepare seventy-five flawless meals a night and charge ninety-five bucks a plate. But in reality, at least in all my places, I've had to push hundreds of meals out the door to keep everyone happily well-paid. As these numbers approach six and seven hundred meals a night, the role of the expeditor requires an intense proficiency similar to that of an air-traffic controller the day before Thanksgiving at O'Hare International.

So, a Saturday night comes along and starts from a quiet still—stocks are simmering, the grill is red hot, prep stations are filled, and the cooks are fueling up with Red Bulls. A ticket comes up on the printer.

It begins.

Fifteen seconds later, another ticket appears, and a minute later, another. Along with an additional expeditor, we organize the tickets on a ticket line, and as cooks finish plates of food, we complete a table and send it off to the dining room. While this is happening, the printer has printed four more tickets. Now two more tables are ready to be sent to the dining room and a specialized team of guys known as food runners—remarkable athletes who are able to balance heavy trays of hot plates, bending and maneuvering like ninjas through crowds of rambling customers—run to serve your dinner to you. When they return to the kitchen, other trays are ready to go and the whole system purrs along with fluency.

An hour into this, I notice the lead sauté cook is getting buried, and we can't complete tables because we're always dragging entrées he makes. Red-faced, he tries to keep up, but he is overloaded—for some ill-fated reason, everything being ordered is coming off his station instead of the typical scenario where items are produced equally by all the cooks. The poor guy is being pounded, falling behind, and running out of everything. As a line cook, and it has happened to all of us, nothing in life is worse than this moment. He pauses a second and looks up at his ticket line. He counts how many ducks he has orders for, and then yells to me in Spanish, "I have thirteen orders and only eight ducks left!"

Fuck. Fuck.

I yell to a runner to go find the servers for the five

tables whose ducks I don't have. Those customers have to order something else.

The pick-up window is now overloaded with plates of food, and we can't run anything because we're still waiting for ducks. The ticket printer continues to punch out tickets one after the other, and the noise level in the kitchen has escalated to a steady yell. Servers are trying to get my attention to tell me their duck-replacements, and I now start to hear from them, with timid respect, that their tables are complaining it's taking too long. They fear saying anything at all to me because they know I'm about to lose my shit.

By now, there are so many tickets fluttering across the ticket holder that it won't hold anymore, and I look at the printer and tickets are strung down to the floor. At one point, as though my brain is trying to prevent a short circuit, the kitchen becomes surreally quiet, like my ears stopped working for a moment, and I just stare at the other expeditor and the five runners whose arms are entangled among themselves trying to grab plates of food.

Then I hear, "We got ducks!"

"Let's go!"

The other cooks jump in to help the buried sauté, but by now, the kitchen timing has broken down—we have lost it. As we push through, ticket by ticket, I am embarrassingly aware that the salads are wilted, the sauces are cooked onto the plates, everything is cold, and food looks like it was plated in an army mess hall. I sigh to myself, shake my head, and tell the runners, "Oh God, just take it."

Forty-five minutes later, as we all slowly emerge from hell, the cooks head outside for a five-minute pre-cleanup break. I can see them leaning against bags of dirty linen, smoking well-earned cigarettes, and talking—maybe about a truck one just bought, or maybe about someone's landlord, or maybe about the new hostess's hefty ass.

One sees me and yells in Spanish, "How many we do?

I yell back, "Five seventy-five."

"Fuckin' shit," he says.

For them, it was a brutal night—but that's all it was. Line cooks are a tough breed. They've been through this before. It is what they do.

As I leave the kitchen, I push through the swinging doors into the dining room with feelings of exhaustion and failure. Most guests are gone by now, thank God, because I don't want to see anyone or talk with anyone. I have a date with a Stoli martini at the bar.

———

One of my Los Angeles restaurants was designed with an indoor-outdoor dining area separated by large sliding doors that, when pushed open, created a beautiful open-air space to dine on those warm, arid nights. However, opening up the dining room also welcomes uninvited guests like flies, or an occasional bird or wasp that would happen to fly through the room.

Of course, it's Saturday night, and the place is packed. It is one of those nights when I feel content that people are loving the food and the energy of the vibrant atmosphere and the smiles on the servers' faces as they buzz around the room. As I stand at the front reception desk telling arrivals it would be just a few minutes for their table to be ready, I could feel the crowd is having a great time.

The main dining room was built with very high ceilings that had long, metal struts running from one side of the building to the other. We hung can-lighting from these struts, giving the ceiling that urban-industrial look that was trendy in those days, creating really cool lighting effects all around the room. As I'm standing there waiting to seat the next table, I notice an odd shadow cast on the entire side of the dining room wall. It looks like an eerie silhouette of an animal with a little, pointed head, a furry body, and a long, whip-like tail—a scene that Hitchcock would have staged, or the haunting nightmare a child would see on their bedroom wall. I turn my head around to find out what could cause such an unnerving shadow and there, resting dauntingly in the middle of a strut, perched high above the festive crowd of the dining room, sits a large, nervous rat. I grab my hostess's shoulder, pull her close to me, and whisper, "Oh my fucking God, look."

With that, it happens.

For a moment, she and I are frozen in horror as time switches to slow motion. In what seems as though it's taking a full minute, the rat falls straight down from the ceiling, like a lead weight, and smacks directly on top of a table of eight who had just begun their dinner. Instantly, my world reverts back to real-time, and over the salsa music playing in the background, I begin to hear shrieks and screams of horror from numerous young women in the room. The rat turns himself upright and scuttles off the table, to the floor, and escapes into the crowded dining room. The table of eight push their chairs back and all stand up. The table next to them stands up. One man puts his arm around his hysterical girlfriend, who was screaming as loud as she could. Two other women run to the ladies' room for some reason, maybe to shelter themselves from further attack or maybe to hyperventilate privately in a stall.

What do you do?

What can you possibly say?

With surprising calm, I walk to the table. By now, they have sat down again but are still very agitated. I stand at their table, pause, and say, "Folks, I am lost for words. All I can do is apologize. I'd also like to buy your dinners for you tonight and another round of cocktails. . . . I'm sure you all need another drink," and I chuckle. And, with the grace of God, they chuckle, as well.

It's amazing how forgiving people can be when you buy them dinner and drinks.

Meanwhile, the rat is nowhere to be found. And don't think for a minute that customers stopped asking me throughout the night if I got it, like it's easy to find and catch a terrified rodent hiding in the maze of booths and decor of a packed restaurant dining room. One unsettled woman was asking every ten minutes, calling me to her table and making a scene every time. I almost said to her, "Yep, I caught the little bastard and hacked it to death with my chef's knife in the kitchen— its blood is splattered all over the wall," just to see her reaction. But instead, to shut her up, as usual, I buy the table drinks. It always works.

The next morning, an exterminator shows up because I knew the little guy was still hiding in the dining room, and I had visions of it running across the floor during service and causing another wave of panic and terror. He told me it would not be easy to catch him, but he would try. For the next three mornings, the exterminator spent a quiet hour alone in the dark dining room. I would peek in and see him slowly creep through the room, like a cat looking for dinner, as though he were trying to understand the psyche of the rat, like the two of them were playing a hide-and-seek game. I had no idea what was taking so long, but on the morning of the fourth day, as he left, he poked his head in my office, paused, smirked, and softly said, "I got him."

And that was it. I didn't ask any questions. I didn't want to know more.

Looking back at the horrors that have unfolded over the years, I can take solace knowing that those events from hell, the catastrophes, the disasters, made me stronger. Strength does not come from easiness. Storms force the roots of a tree to grow deeper. I now realize that these struggles changed me for the better.

ROUTINE

*"What you do every day matters more than
what you do once in a while."*

GRETCHEN RUBIN

Well, now I'm in it—deep in it. I find myself working like a dog every day to throw a dinner party for hundreds of people, and at the end of the night, after accomplishing this feat, making sure people are happy as they walk out the door, excited to come back, everyone buzzed and smiling, I realize that tomorrow I must start again. Every day, there's another party to throw.

Still in the infancy of restaurant life, I am in the constant throes of trying to build my business and fall victim to the incessant barrage of advertising salespeople. I've never been one to believe that restaurant advertising is effective—to me, it's always been a waste of money. Few people, if any, try a restaurant because they see a tiny little ad with a cool logo or a photo of some food-styled entrée, but advertising and public relations firms try to coerce me into spending considerable money—money that's precious in my infancy—to buy listings and ads. Often, with a purchased ad, the magazine will "review" my business. I must provide, at no cost, a full-course meal including alcohol, usually to a group of four, and one of them will write a favorable article about my business that they claim hordes of people will read. In the beginning, this sounds great, but wolves come in, as they often do, and I find that they are really just trying to find subject matter for their obscure publications or blogs. The articles do more for them than me, and I rarely see any turnout from what they write.

Instead, people try a new restaurant because someone they know went there and told them what they thought—either *OMG, I went to the best place last night,* or *I went to that new restaurant last night and it sucked.* New business is built on referral. If a guest leaves happy and excited, had fun, and ate really great food, they will return, often with others. People love to show off a new discovery. It's the first sign I'm on the right path—when people come with their friends and go out of their way to introduce them to me.

As the evenings pass, mercifully, routines form and take hold. I try to delegate to my illustrious staff specific responsibilities that, if followed precisely, lend themselves to a nonissue day—but absolutely and without question, every single day, someone, without fail, fucks something up. And when they fuck something up, I must fix it.

I think of myself as the conductor of the orchestra. I never play a specific instrument, because if I do, I have no idea what everyone else is doing; instead, my head is down in my own world. This is why, as chef, I never work a particular cook station. I need to walk around and observe, but it goes without question that if a cook no-shows on me, I am there in the trenches making pastas or grilling steaks until eleven.

My job is to make sure that everyone else does his or her job.

As a chef, much time is spent trying to understand customers' palates and what they like to eat. If you can predict this, then you have a winner. Your menu works. But if you end up serving something only *you* want to eat, like your mother's beef stroganoff on noodles, that vomit-like stew of shaved beef and cream—no matter how well it is prepared—then you are going to lose. Few people want to eat that. Restaurant food has become very sophisticated.

What a chef personally enjoys eating should have

little to do with what is served on a menu. This is the hardest concept for chefs to grasp. Many imprudent menu writers are just hardheaded and fill menus with awful choices. It is why someone sits in a restaurant holding a menu and ponders, "Hmm, I don't know what I want." It is not because everything sounds so mouth-watering—it's the opposite. A good chef listens to their audience, is aware of what sells, and regularly reinvents his or her food.

Two things are important—someone's reaction when they *read* what is on the menu, and someone's reaction when they *taste* what they ordered.

And God knows chefs can forget about servers informing them of a customer's remarks. It doesn't hap-pen. If a guest says to the server, "Let the chef know that . . ." —it usually dies there. Servers care about how much someone tips and not much more. Chefs and cooks rarely hear whether you liked the sea bass or whether the soup is a little salty. And, if I ask a server, "Did they like it?" They usually lie because they don't know. Instead, I hear, "Ah, oh yeah."

I roll my eyes and walk away.

I suppose this is a good time to write a few words about servers and their sole purpose in life: tips. First, you must know that servers want to spend as little time in a restaurant as possible, and for the few hours a day they're there, they want to earn as much as they can.

When a guy pays his check and leaves a restaurant, without fail his server has checked how much he's tipped by the time he gets to the front door. If he has left a zero tip—and yes, some people do—I never have an issue with permitting the server to run him down and ask if there was a problem. Some customers get pissed that a server would stoop this low, and I have had a fair share come back to me, blabbering in my face how insulted they are that the server confronted them. But, you know, this is how a server makes a living, and I don't care how shitty of a job he or she did, you should give them something. They still had to put on a happy face and stand stoic at the table, listening to some jerk deliberate fifty menu items, obsessing about ordering the filet mignon, and whether he should order it medium or medium-rare, or medium-rare plus, or maybe medium-rare but charred on the outside, or no, medium is better—all the while five other tables need attention, trays of cocktails at the bar need to be carried to other tables, the chef wants them in the kitchen, and their bladder is about to explode. Then there's the table who orders one single item every time the server returns to the table. "I'll have a Chardonnay." The server gets it, places it on the table, then another person says, "Can I get a Stoli and soda?" The server returns with the drink, then someone says, "Can I see a menu?" Then someone says, "Can we start with a bowl of edamame?" This behavior continues, treating the server as a personal assistant—then, at the end of the meal, the server opens the check presenter and sees they left a whopping 12 percent tip.

What many don't realize is only about half of that tip actually goes to the server. The other half is divided among all the other people running around—the bussers, the food runners, the bartenders, the barbacks, the hosts, and sometimes even the dishwasher. So, if someone stiffs a server because he forgot a salad, or because he was charged for the extra anchovies that a manager wouldn't remove from the check, it's the whole service staff who is screwed over. Most servers take pride in their jobs—there's a lot of competition and they know the next résumé that arrives at the restaurant could be their replacement. When they fail at a table, it's the management's fault—either they hired a server with too little experience, or they buried the guy with too many tables.

Back in the kitchen, the hours that a restaurant is *not* open are spent preparing for when it *is* open. A big part of my typical day is troubleshooting food deliveries. They *never* come in right—something is always missing, not what was ordered or expected, or poor quality. And, when my delivery is dropped off, I am frequently bestowed with a mystery item that is not on the invoice, something like a bag of Coney Island corn dog mix.

Where the hell did that come from? These surprises are often thrown back in the storeroom by an unknowing cook and are discovered weeks later. Storerooms and walk-in freezers always contain dead soldiers that mysteriously appeared from nowhere.

Keeping a full kitchen staff is also a relentless challenge. It is easier to find a NASA system engineer than to find a good line cook. Someone is always quitting. I have just spent months training some guy, and he's fast, clean, doesn't steal, doesn't drink, and doesn't bitch. Then he shows up Friday afternoon and tells me his mother is sick in Guadalajara and he is heading back in the morning. These kinds of things happen so often that I often keep one extra cook around as backup, squeezing in shifts for him as I can. I sometimes hire someone who drops by the kitchen to see if we're hiring, even if I really don't need him.

A typical morning starts when the deliveries arrive. As they are checked in and put away, I walk to my station, Japanese filleting knife in one hand and a food-crusted cell phone in the other. The daily production sheet is being tallied and the squad of prep cooks is poised to go.

Then it starts.

A busy restaurant kitchen is never big enough, unless you work in a casino or on a cruise ship, and prep cooks have developed an amazing ability to work on top of each other. They can manage to dice a sack of onions in a twelve-inch square space on a cutting board and, while doing so, have three pots of various things cooking on the stove, trays of something else roasting in the oven, mounds of frozen shrimp and squid thawing under water, and pizza dough kneading in the mixer. Then, out of nowhere, without fail, one runs over to me and says, "We don't have ginger."

"Why not? I saw ginger yesterday. It was there. What are you making?"

"The shrimp filling for the wontons."

Fuck. I realize you cannot make wonton filling without ginger—I dig cash out of my pocket with my fish-scented hand and send her off to buy ginger. As I turn the corner, the dishwasher says to me (in Spanish), "They never picked up the garbage yesterday. The bin is overfull. Where should I put all these bags of garbage?"

"Why the fuck wasn't the garbage picked up?"

I call the garbage company, a recorded voice puts me on hold, and I switch to speakerphone so I can fillet fish while I wait. Five minutes pass and another call rings into my phone—it's the meat vendor. I realize I am at the ordering cut-off time, and I have to order. I hang up from being on hold with the garbage company to take his call and place the meat order. The pace in the kitchen is hurried and rushed. It is now 2 p.m. Line cooks are arriving in an hour, and I still have to finish the soup, check the curry sauce that is simmering, and get the rest of the pots off the stovetops. Once these night cooks show up at 3 p.m., I know to be clear of the cooking line area—it now becomes their turf—and a territory war starts if I'm not.

The afternoon is coming to an end, and I head to the office to regroup and phone in my food orders for the next day. A line cook comes into the office and tells me that Alfredo is not here yet. "Where the fuck is he?" I call his cell, but it goes right to voicemail.

"Shit. Well, try to get his station set up. I'll be right there," I say.

Another line cook runs into the office and tells me there is no truffle aioli. I realize I forgot to make it. "Damn it. Okay, I'll make it."

After the aioli is made, I head to Alfredo's station. Dozens of people are hurrying everywhere. An early ticket comes up on the printer; it's a crab cake and, of course, it's something made at Alfredo's station.

Fuck, he's not here. I have to make the crab cake.

As I heat up a skillet, Alfredo, red-faced and sweating, comes running into the kitchen. "Why the fuck are you late?"

"My car overheated," he gabbles in Spanish.

I shake my head and say, "You need a crab cake—now. Let's go," and I walk away.

Heading back to the office, I notice bags of garbage

lying on the floor. "Oh shit, I have to call them back," But it's now after 5 p.m. and the company is closed.

Fuck.

"Just try to stack these bags on top of the garbage that's already in the dumpster—maybe they'll empty it in the morning," I tell the dishwasher in Spanish, but I know for damn sure the company will not empty an overfull dumpster.

I think to myself, *I'll call them in the morning*—and I do.

A chef must have a good memory.

If everyone does exactly what they were supposed to, my day is cool and painless. But it never happens. Chefs and restaurant managers incessantly put out fires, one after the next, day after day. Some days, there are few. Other days, it's the burning of Rome.

By just about 5 p.m. in most restaurants, the prep staff heads home for the night and the cooks have brought their stations up, ready to cook. When service begins, the chef generally strolls around the kitchen, up and down the cooking line, shoulder to shoulder with the cooks, and notices everything—how hot they preheat a skillet, how much salt the grill cook is throwing on a steak, how thinly the onions are sliced for a salad—everything. Each cook executes his or her particular plates, under the scrutinizing watch of the chef, and places them in a heated pick-up window ready to be carried off to a table. As these finished plates sit and await transportation, the chef typically paces up and down the line, like a drill sergeant during a troop inspection, and with an offhand glance and a raise of his eyebrows, assesses each plate. Some people have what my dad coined "the eyes." This is the innate ability, a peculiarity that some people are born with, to instantly notice detail. Not everyone is so blessed, or perhaps cursed, but those who have it can take a mental snapshot and, in a flash, catch something out of sorts. A chef with "the eyes" will immediately notice that cherry tomatoes are missing from an eight-ingredient salad or that the skin isn't crispy enough on a pan-fried striped bass. Dining room managers with "the eyes" will walk past a table and quickly see that the server neglected to remove an empty cocktail glass or that a place setting is missing a fork. A good bartender with "the eyes" immediately knows the moment a guest sips the last of their cocktail and is ready for a second.

The chef gathers a wealth of information with just that glance—what we cannot determine is how something will taste, and to do so, as you may know, cooks and chefs universally employ, most conveniently, his or her finger. A quick dab on a sauce, then to the tongue, and a seasoned palate is fed as much tasting information as will usually suffice.

Well, I guess this is where I must tell you what everyone wants to know but is always afraid to ask. This is where I share the sordid inner practices of a restaurant kitchen, the unspoken truths of those who commit food crimes to an unsuspecting public. If the thoughts of a cook tasting your sauce with his finger makes you cringe, then you should probably eat at home from this point on.

The European kitchens I worked in during my years as a *stage* had a different set of cleanliness standards than do our domestic health departments. In France, there was often a dog or two cleaning scraps from the floor, and absolutely everyone smoked. The kitchens were designed with stovetops and ovens around a center island used to plate the food. As the cooks worked using both hands, they always had cigarettes hanging from their faces and the long ashes dangling at the tips would just fall to the floor. If the ash happened to drop onto a plate ready to be served, a quick blow of air from their lips cleaned it off, no problem. I saw it many times.

Why most food sins happen, why cooks do what they do, usually arise from the pressure of having to hurry. Hurry, hurry, fast, fast—that's the mojo is a busy restaurant kitchen. A cook finishes a beautiful *cioppino* in a sauté pan filled with four prawns, three scallops, and clams, and is just about to serve it all in a hot bowl. The expeditor is yelling for him to hurry, he needs the plate to complete a table. With the sauté pan in his left hand and tongs in his right, the cook makes one final flip of the seafood and out flies one of the prawns to the floor. In a continuous, nonstop, sweeping motion, as though it is planned choreography, the cook swoops down to the floor mat, grabs the prawn with his tongs, and returns it to the pan. One more flip of the *cioppino* and it is promptly served in the bowl. This is an example of the infamous two-second rule universally followed by cooks—anything that hits the floor for less than two seconds is salvageable and good to go.

In the kitchens of some very remarkable restaurants in which I have done time, I have watched in horror as chefs, in an attempt to hurry, toss prime filet mignon in the deep-fat fryer to cut cooking time. Or grill cooks who use their body weight to press the blood out of a steak, turning it from medium-rare to well in just seconds. At a grand hotel in the French Quarter of New Orleans, as a young apprentice, I was stationed in the back pantry, pumping out salads and shrimp cocktails for this stoic institution. Along the back wall, behind the hot cooking line, were a group of microwaves that had the sole purpose of cooking lobsters—live lobsters. I used to cringe as old, rough line cooks would grab a lobster out of a tank, tail flipping in their hand, hustle back to the microwave, pop open the door, throw the poor bastard inside, slam the door, and push number

10. Ten minutes later, when the bell went off, they'd return and pull out a perfectly steaming-hot red lobster. As I stood and made my salads through the night's service, my only solace from this heinous act came from the rumble of the updrafts that muffled any imagined cries I might have heard.

Dad used to say the less you know, the better you sleep.

When you think about it, it really wasn't that long ago that we had to kill our own dinner. My grandparents did it, and a large part of the world's population still does it. During my *stage* in Europe, live chickens arriving at the kitchen door were commonplace and fish were frequently delivered still in water. At one trattoria in Italy, the grill cook would grab a live trout from a bag and hold it from flipping around on his hot grill with a brick wrapped in foil. The practice of producing *foie gras*, the buttery goose liver made by French farmers who nail goose feet to wooden planks and force-feed them with plastic tubes to enflame their livers was so atrocious that serving the liver was actually banned in many US states, available only via the culinary underground. My grandmother told me that, as a girl, her friend's mother would kill a chicken by putting its head in a door jam, turn away, slam the door shut, and then run out of the room. She'd return minutes later to find the dead bird on the floor.

But let me tell you this: In my half-century of kitchen

work, along with the hundreds of cooks with whom I have labored, not even once, not even maybe, have I ever seen anyone spit in someone's food. I'm really not sure where this notion originated, maybe just the lore of urban legend, maybe just the paranoia of some deserving patron, but kindly know that there most definitely exists a vein of human decency and respect for their craft that all kitchen cooks share. Despite the poor conditions, despite the shitty pay, and despite the grueling hours, they have chosen to cook for a living. The worst you'll usually get from them for sending your entrée back to the kitchen for the third time is a mouthful of vulgarities about you, and probably about your mother.

The gruesome tales of kitchen accidents and mangled carnage I have witnessed and to which I have been first responder are something I try to forget. Rarely a day goes by without an insignificant nick of someone's finger, nothing a little Band-Aid can't fix. But working quickly with razor-sharp knives, slicers, shredders, boiling water, and hot oil splashing out of skillets can be the cause of serious injuries, and all experienced cooks have taken their turn as victim. Sparing you the grisly details, there have been too times in my life that I've wrapped someone's hand in kitchen towels and a plastic garbage bag and flew through red lights to get them to an emergency room. When the subject of these accidents comes up during a moment of downtime in a restaurant kitchen, everyone gladly shares an episode, a horror they witnessed or heard about, one more terrifying than the next, always trying to out-shock the previous raconteur. The scars on a cook's hands and arms tell the real story.

———————

A time came in my life when I found myself in the throes of a metamorphosis—the chef, the guy who had spent all his time in the kitchen, was changing into something else. I was becoming a restauranteur.

I was cooking less. I had walked out of the kitchen and into the world of business—payroll, accounting, taxes, licensing, handling employees' issues, repairs and maintenance, promotion, advertising, and more headaches after headaches. I did not make the soup myself anymore; instead, I would show one of the boys how to make it, then I showed him how to *taste* it; he had to learn what "good" was. I still did the daily ordering for food and supplies because it kept me mindful of how much money I was spending, and I still wrote the menu, but my days as a working chef were gently fading. Fortunately, I was pretty good at keeping a top-notch kitchen staff around that knew what they were doing. I understood what it took to keep them happy. I looked at them as family and they always had my back.

You respect them, and they respect you. That's how it works.

As I worked in the kitchen, those swinging kitchen doors always protected me. They served as the great barrier separating the comfort of my kitchen from that mysterious, alternate universe—the public. Through those doors, reality changes. You must look right, speak right, smile, be courteous, and become self-deprecating to that great enigma known as customer service. In the kitchen, everyone listens to me. In the dining room, I must listen to everyone, and this artificial, subservient behavior begins the moment a guest walks in the front door.

Working behind a host stand in a busy restaurant should be a social studies prerequisite in college. It is actually quite enjoyable since most folks arrive cheerful and excited to visit. But it soon becomes apparent to me that the public basket always contains a sour apple or two, and soon enough, I am challenged—someone claims they made a reservation that I don't have.

The house is packed. People are flowing into the restaurant in an endless stream, one after the next. A middle-aged woman with expensive earrings and too much makeup stands in front of me.

I say, "Hi there, what's the name on the reservation?"

She pauses a moment, looks me right in the eye with no emotion, and says, "Mrs. Gifford." I begin the search for her name in the database. There is no Gifford.

"Could it be another name?"

"No. Gifford. Party of four. Seven o'clock."

I say, "I'm sorry, I don't have that name. Did you make the reservation online or did you call the restaurant?"

This is the defining moment. I carefully study her body language and expression before she answers. I make direct eye contact with her. If she says "online," then I am golden, since it just became *her* mistake if there is no reservation in the system. But instead, she pauses for a moment and says, "No, I called this afternoon."

"Who did you speak with?" I politely respond.

She says, "He didn't tell me his name."

Now I know she's lying. The only person answering phones all day was my hostess, a woman. Mrs. Gifford suspects I am on to her. At this point, I lean forward and politely but firmly explain to her that only my hostess was there all day, no guy.

Again, she pauses again and says, "Well, I know I made it."

Had we been on the other side of the swinging doors in the seclusion of my kitchen, I would have said, "Why the fuck are you lying to me? Just ask for a table, be honest, and I'll get you in." But here, in the world of self-righteous behavior and manners, I smile and say, "So, you are four. . . . Let me take a look, ma'am. Let's see what we can do."

So are the ways of the front-of-the-house, that unique social setting that defies natural human interaction in favor of the subservient practice of apologetic ass kissing, and no one on Earth is better at this fine art than servers.

Servers, or *waiters* as they used to be called, are a rare breed. They are filled with other dreams beyond waiting tables, and they often act as though they are doing you a favor for showing up. They want to serve as many tables as possible in as short of time as possible—make money and get out—that's their mojo. Though they are all hired to do the same job, their personalities are all quite different. Most are easygoing and play well with others, like different breeds of dogs, typically good-natured customer-service employees. But there is always one who likes to start shit. They are easy to recognize and, like a grade-school teacher who has a pain in the ass kid in the class, I grab the troublemaker server and throw him in detention. I have had many conversations with servers that begin, "What the hell's wrong with you?!" They back down because they know they're wrong, and they know how much money they make working for me.

Everything always comes down to the money.

The weekly scheduling of servers is daunting. They complain they either work too much or not enough. If I schedule someone on Monday, they must swap shifts with someone else because Monday they have "something." Others cannot start early because their husband does not get home to babysit until 5:30; others, cannot work on Sunday, it is the only day their wife doesn't work; others have class three nights a week; others cannot take tables at the end of the night since they work somewhere else at 7 a.m. and have to get up early. I look at them and think *I'm here every day from noon until midnight, and you can't commit to a five-hour shift, four nights a week?*

But I know if I give them what *they* want, they will give me what *I* want.

As is always the case with employees, a few illustrious members of the team will remain in my life for many years. We worked through many shifts together, side-by-side side, managing the stress with laughter, and spent numerous post-shift Saturday nights around the bar, when customers have gone home, drinking wine and sharing stories about how sweet the lady was at table 12 that night or what a dick the guy was at table 30.

Laugher helps us sleep at night.

Why is the restaurant business notoriously the most brutal of all? Is it really? Well, statistically, there is no doubt. When a new restaurant opens, only about 10 percent last for more than one year. And of those that make it a year, only about 50 percent go on for another year. Anything more than three years, and I know I'm golden. That means what I am doing is working, the recipe is right—and it just may, someday, be considered an institution.

This is why it's tough:

Whenever I open a new restaurant, I forfeit my social life. Customers always expect me to be there and to make a fuss when they show up. No longer will I spend holidays with my family, I will miss my pets, rarely play golf, live with a cell phone in my hand, and work fifteen-hour days—even on a Tuesday—and must muster the energy and stamina of a teenager. It is physically demanding; I am on my feet the whole day and I must always smile and keep people happy, even if I'm trying to cope with some personal trauma myself. When that curtain goes up and I'm in the light, I have to be on. And I must be a psychologist since every single person on my staff has an impulsive personality and a unique set of personal ordeals and traumas that they regularly bring to work every day—I never know what I am going to get until they show up. They will walk through the door red-eyed from crying, or high, or drunk, or they will say, "I have really bad diarrhea, but I'll be okay." Then they spend most of the night in the restroom.

Perhaps most challenging of all, I must continually generate my product from scratch. It is not as though I'm selling a manufactured electronic device, or some cool T-shirts from a stocked inventory, or a web design service. I depend on people to create two products that

I sell—the food, and the experience of eating the food—and it must be repeated every single day of the year. It never lets up.

Never.

One day I have to wash dishes, another I have to clean out a puke-filled urinal, and another I might get hit in the face trying to break up a bar fight. Emotionally and psychologically, I must prepare myself for brutal criticism, either to my face or on social media. My business is subject to countless events that occur in life by chance, such as a wicked storm that blows in, or a power failure when you have three hundred reservations. And of course, there are nights that none of my "regulars" come in—they instead stay home to watch the Academy Awards, or the Dodgers in a semifinal game, or the election results—and in the meantime, I stand at work praying someone shows up. I must still pay my staff, who are leaning against the wall doing nothing, plus I have twenty-five marinated pork chops and bags of shrimp cocktail that have to be sold.

When a business involves the public that must physically walk around, like in a restaurant, or an airline, or at sports arena, mishaps and accidents occur regularly. People frequently stumble on their own feet, or over a step, or on the leg of a chair and fall to the floor, lying there moaning about their ankle until a passing server or busboy helps them stand again. Others choke and run up to the host stand in hopes for a Heimlich maneuver, or get cut on a glass, or just stand up and out of nowhere faint at their table. I have discovered people passed out in the restroom in a pool of blood, hitting their head on the floor as they fell. Or people running out the front door as they experience an allergic reaction, or others convinced they're having a heart attack, call 911, and to my surprise, paramedics rush in the front door pushing a gurney with IV bags into the crowded restaurant asking who called. Then, sadly, there are those incidents when elderly customers don't make it to the restroom in time, leaving quite an embarrassing mess for employees to clean up in the dining room, at the host stand, or at the bar. It has happened many times.

Restaurants are plagued with inordinate failure, because the people who open them frankly do not have experience. These entrepreneurs are good at raising money, selling the dream, have a great love for food and the art of dining, and often think their convivial personality floundering about the dining room will be enough to keep the place packed. But it is a business with complicated financial parameters that must be diligently monitored. The margins are as small as any business, and restaurants generally pay last week's bills with this week's money. One or two slow weeks, and money stress ensues. Taxes are high; minimum wage *for tipped employees* in most states, especially California, is ridiculously inflated; you are inundated with government rules and regulations; and you cannot get through a single week without being hit by an unexpected bill for some off-the-wall unexpected expense.

Surprise bills come at you like stray bullets.

Then there are the repairs. No one plans for a refrigerator motor to burn up, or an oven to not light, or an ice machine to quit, or a mixer to jam, or a printer to go offline, or a drain to clog—the list endlessly goes on. Everything just keeps breaking. A busy restaurant that has been around for a while is in a constant state of repair—expensive repair.

Restaurant owners know the truth. They have walked through hell.

So why would anyone want to open a restaurant?

This is why:

Throughout the years, whether working at my dad's places as a teenager, consulting for other restauranteurs, or running my own businesses, I have probably been involved with about fifty restaurants. I am not new to this life. Something inside of me keeps me doing it again and again. This addiction is common with restaurateurs. Even when restaurant owners suffer painful, humiliating failures or financial bankruptcies, I have often seen them rise from the ashes and quickly spawn a new project. For all of us, it begins romantically. Inspiration is triggered by a photograph, or from a new cookbook you find, or from a chat with another dreamer who found the perfect real estate, or through a life-changing adventure you experience on a journey through Asia. The exhilaration that comes from conceiving a new restaurant once again starts stirring in us like caffeine in the morning. The obsession begins—we sell the concept to our project team with passion and conviction and the story builds. Before you know it, we are signing a lease. Together with the mastermind, we raise capital, design, construct, and subsequently, one day, open and operate our collective vision. It is teamwork, and it is one of the great pleasures of the business—you are part of a team set toward a common goal.

Even though I certainly try to establish a routine, it never quite happens. On the contrary, as a business owner, I can make adaptations at my whim. I can vary the décor, I can hire new staff, I can refocus the menu, or I can change the dining room mood with music and lighting. It is an ongoing evolution and gives me boundless creativity. As a chef, not a day goes by that I don't tweak a dish; maybe it is the way it is plated, maybe I just adjust the sauce, or maybe I pull it from the menu and feature something seasonal instead. I am in charge of the product and the direction it takes.

A busy restaurant is a grand social event. With time, I recognize countless faces as they walk through the door. I greet them with a smile or a hug and am often genuinely excited to see them. It is a great mixture of people, from attorneys and celebrities to plumbers and retirees. I often hear how glad they are to be back, and when they share a story from their recent trip to India, it sparks me thinking again about traveling somewhere myself. Or perhaps they rave about the lobster spring roll we served last week—it was best thing they ever had. As I wander around the room and chat with the crowd, the sum of all these minute-long conversations leaves me enriched and fulfilled.

The fast-paced excitement of each day keeps me young. There is little time to get lost in lonely depression. I do not sit at a desk and tap a pencil or sink into the abyss of social media or cable news for hours. My brain runs as though it is on jet fuel, making decisions and dousing fires as they start. Nothing is stagnant about my life.

Everyone who works in a restaurant is an adrenaline junkie.

As my own boss, I do not have to listen to another boss's imprudence. I pick my staff, I pick my product, and I am ultimately responsible for what goes on in my own bank account. I do not have to wait all year for that two-week vacation in August when someone else permits me to travel the world, and I don't have to call in sick one day if what I really want to do is go for a hike on the mountain. No one tells me what I must do.

Vendors often arrive with gifts and samples. In a busy restaurant, few days pass without someone giving me something. They drop off a bag of organic peaches from a local farm they had visited or a bottle of a wine from a promising new vineyard. There always seems to be bottles of wine everywhere to try, and there are refrigerators full of steaks and vegetables for me to loot if I feel like cooking dinner at home for a couple of friends.

But it is really all about the customers.

A gorgeous feeling of peace and accomplishment comes from the praise I often receive. It is profound and nurturing. How wonderful I feel when I see the joy in someone's eyes as they first taste the soup, or when they tell me they've brought a friend in to try the pork chop they had last week, or when customers humbly thank me for just having opened the place. There have been times that a table has asked to see me and when I got there, they all started to applaud. And there have been uncountable times that I hear praise about employees and what a remarkable job they do. I receive flowers, handwritten notes, and many emails from thoughtful, gentle people whose lives are touched by a special dinner they had. There are special birthdays and anniversaries and memorials. My eyes well up with stories they recall about the last meal they shared with a friend who just passed away and how they want to have his eulogy at what was his favorite restaurant.

Betty and her husband, Bill, were frequent guests, the kind of folks who knew everyone at the bar, moving from person to person, saying hi, laughing and joking as they'd go. They were a fabulous couple and visited every weekend for as long as I can remember. They defined what are referred to as "regulars." One evening, Betty pulled me aside, looked me right in the eyes, and softly whispered, "Bill has cancer." Her eyes welled up and she began to cry. As I hugged her, she said, "They give him just a few months. I don't know what I am going to do without him." I was devastated and tried to assure her to be strong for him and to know that we'd always be there for her. Over the next couple of months, Betty and Bill would still come by each weekend, but you could see how Bill's treatment was taking its toll. Then one weekend, I noticed they weren't there. About a month later, just as happy hour was getting started, Betty walked in the front door alone and stood quietly to the side. When I saw her, I knew what had happened. We hugged for a minute as she cried and cried and told me she lost Bill that week. As time passed, Betty began visiting the restaurant again on weekends, and then one night, when she and I were chatting alone, she leaned into me and said, "You know, I never told you, but after Bill was cremated, I brought some of his ashes here and when no one what looking, sprinkled them in the planters all around the patio." She smiled, "That way I know he's always here with me."

It is really all so very moving.

Kind people abound.

Through all of the long hours and struggles shines a beautiful side of humanity in this business, and not a day goes by that I am not made aware of it. There are frequent blessings.

YELP

*"There is only one way to avoid criticism:
Do nothing, say nothing, and be nothing."*

ARISTOTLE

Here we go.

Anyone who knows me is well aware of my deep, guttural loathing of the online review company Yelp. Chefs and restaurateurs universally detest both the company and the elite group of people, referred to as Yelpers, who partake in the charade. The company's formidable review platform allows anyone—absolutely anyone—to sign on to the site and, for free, post reckless comments about an unfounded personal experience they had with someone's business. There is no screening, no vetting, no support, and no verification of the poster's authenticity. What one reads could be a complete lie—a bunch of made-up garbage that your "ex" posts on your business's page because she's pissed you dumped her.

Next what happens is that some lady from Wisconsin reads the bad review and says to her husband, "Oh my, I won't go there. That place sounds horrible."

Such is how it works. You get the picture.

There is good in the restaurant business, and there is bad. This is the ugly.

It's not just Yelp. There are others. But it was Yelp who first got my attention since Yelp, unlike the rest, allows a business owner to *respond*. What these companies hope for is that businesses advertise with them in an attempt to improve their online status—their esteemed *star rating*. However, though Yelp claims that such advertising does not affect a business's rank in the rating system, I don't buy it. It may not actually factor in to how many stars you get, but Yelp uses complicated sorting algorithms that can increase, or decrease, the exposure your business gets and who appears at the top of a search list. Yelp even uses their computers to pick and choose which reviews to display, hiding both bad and a lot of good reviews that legitimate customers post. These online review sites are there to take advertising dollars—certainly not to help someone choose the best island resort to visit or best steak house to try.

Over the past few years, hospitality culture, mainly due to the onslaught of novice cell phone critics, has put way too much faith and credibility into these sites. If a server forgets someone's cocktail, the next day you find a post about the horrific experience they had, often filled with issues and exaggerations, how inept and rude the server was, how the restaurant did not comp anything, the food sucked and, without fail, these rants always end with the proverbial ". . . and I'll never be back,"—the ultimate slam to a business owner. These wits are the epitome of entitled, negative energy.

And so began my obsession with Yelp, because you see, when these episodes would occur, I always knew precisely and honestly what happened. I was there. I experienced the truth.

For example, if some dude sends a fifty-dollar steak back to the kitchen because he orders it medium-rare and claims it was medium, the server typically notifies me. It is the rule. I would check the steak in the bright light of the kitchen (instead of what the customer saw in the dark dining room), and see, in fact, it is a perfect medium-rare—perfect.

And I am right.

I know what I'm talking about because, for most of my adult life, I have cooked steaks. Thousands of them. I know that medium-rare means the steak has a red but warm center. My grill guy is a rock star. He is the best.

If a steak is sent back to the bright light of the kitchen, he runs over to the plate, sticks his chest out, and aggressively checks it out. It is his baby.

At this point, we all throw our hands up in the air, shake our heads, and say, "Fuck that guy."

But—to avoid confrontation, I make the guy a new steak, just to appease his self-righteous ass, and so I can get back to other business. It is how most restaurants do things. The new steak goes back to the dining room, cooked exactly like the first, and we all move on. The dumbass now nods to his server that he is happy.

Whoever said the customer was always right never worked in a restaurant. If fact, the customer is usually wrong.

The next morning, sipping my coffee at my computer, I get a Yelp notification that we received a new review on their site. I take a look and, sure enough, the dumbass had posted a paragraph on how his night was ruined since we mis-cooked his dinner and he had to sit there for a half hour waiting for a new steak to be grilled. He writes, "Even my second steak was over-cooked, but I didn't want to wait for another . . . this place should learn how to cook, I order steaks all the time, and I can't believe they have the audacity to charge me $50 for an overcooked piece of leather. Plus, they didn't take anything off the check for my inconvenience. From now on, I'm spending my money elsewhere."

As I read this, my fingers start to tap my desk.

My caffeine-fueled blood bubbles. If this guy walked into the room at that moment, I would likely attack him.

Then I notice at the top of the page that he rates us with *one star*. Out of five, we get one. It is a rating that means the business is despicable and should be avoided at all costs. He had not considered how friendly the hosts were and how he was given a great table, or the beautiful dining room he was sitting in, or the accommodating server, or how often the bussers filled his water glass, or the perfectly shaken martini he sucked down.

It is one star.

Period.

And what makes matters worse is that this bogus one-star rating is then factored into my *overall* rating, which is displayed next to the name of my business *everywhere*; not only on Yelp's site but on a host of other reckless internet sites—it is all unnervingly connected, like some alien with interwoven tentacles. Google the name of anyone's business and it comes up with a star rating right next to it. I am vulnerable, defenseless, and publicly judged by a select neurotic few who hide deep inside the internet.

So, this is what happens. There is no checkpoint that deems anyone's review authentic. Someone does not even have to eat in a restaurant to write a review. It could be 100 percent a lie. To get an account on Yelp, anyone in the public can just post a fictitious screen name and what city they live in (like anyone cares), and that's it. Then it's open season.

Now, Yelp does offer me the right to contest someone's review. I must choose from a drop-down menu of seven reasons why they should *consider* removing it, but it is just one more pathetic insult from Yelp since I *always* receive a form email from them a day later that says, "After careful evaluation, we have decided not to remove this content at this time." And there is no reply address.

That is it.

How fucking offensive is that? Careful evaluation? What does that mean? Depending on which of the seven reasons I picked, my business was just reevaluated by either a computer algorithm or some guy in a room in Bangladesh. Some covert loser just posted an outright lie about my business on this website for the whole world to see, and they take no responsibility. There is nothing I can do. Their legal department maintains that the public has the right to post what they want.

Let's go one step further. Yelp is unique in that it allows a business owner to *respond* to a review. Not all companies permit this, but they do. To do so, I must sign on to another site, called Yelp for Business Owners. To join this site, Yelp vets me. They verify everything about me. They even phone my business to make sure it is real and confirm I am the legal owner, and *I must post a photo of myself with my name.* They make a great effort to verify everything about the owner of the business, but the people they let post reviews could be Santa Claus or the Easter Bunny.

Then, this is the best—if I attempt to respond to someone's slanderous review, windows pop up all over my screen with warnings by Yelp *to be nice.* They suggest I *thank* the reviewer for their feedback, keep my comments positive, and resist temptation to argue. I should tell them how I will change things for the better and invite them back. They ask me to essentially kiss their ass for trashing my business—it is all my fault, and I must humbly ask for forgiveness.

As I click through the site, I am astonished how business owners conform to these recommendations. Some of the responses I read make me want to hurl. They are gooey and sweet, bubbling over with apologies and explanations from despairing business owners. They ask for mercy, promising to do better the next time. "Please come back, let me buy you dinner." How can I possibly respond like that after reading something such as what that dumbass wrote about his steak? Instead, I choose to walk away. I turned off my computer and headed into work, where I would spend the next ten hours of my day trying to make hundreds of people happy.

Day after day, reviews come in, and some are just relentless, especially if the business is new. The public tries it out then feels the dire necessity to post a mock–Siskel and Ebert critique, hiding behind a screen name, either praising my work or tearing me down. It is not good enough anymore for them to just tell their friends about their experiences. It takes on validity when it is posted, almost as though they think humanity is being served by their astute advice. Now please know that not all reviews are unscrupulous, and I must admit I am quite revitalized when I read how happy I have made some people and what a good time they had. Healthy criticism can come from anyone, even your mother. But a business owner's nature is such that we remember the bad.

A restaurant can serve hundreds of exuberant guests, and at the end of the night, the staff sits around talking about the one guy who caused a scene.

Fast-forward a couple of years.

I had pretty much quit reading customers' online opinions of my work and that of my employees. The good was good, but the bad just upset me too much.

Then one day, it all changed.

I had a hostess who worked for me about a year. She was maybe nineteen, wide-eyed and newly planted to the west coast. She came from a small, rural town in Indiana and had a sweet purity and innocence about her. One evening, in a packed restaurant, she attempted to walk a customer to his table when he stopped, turned to her, and started yelling that he was promised another table. She was taken back by his aggression, became disheveled, and just froze. He walked away from her and ran back to the front desk, shouting that she was incompetent and blah, blah, blah—he demanded a different table. We gave him what he wanted, assured the hostess that it was okay, told her to calm down and to just move on with the night.

Sure enough, the next morning, as I sat with my coffee, there was a big, fat, one-star review on Yelp from this guy about how rude my hostess was. He continued that she was homely and dreadfully ugly, had stringy, poorly dyed hair, wore too much whorelike makeup, etc., etc. I thought, *God, I can't believe someone would write this.*

That evening during service, talk of the review came up at the host stand. I stepped away for a moment, and when I returned, I found my hostess reading the review on her phone, just crying and crying. There stood this innocent teenager, crushed and devastated.

I walked back to my office and pulled up this guy's review on Yelp. When I clicked that I wanted to respond, I got the usual barrage of windows from Yelp warning me to be nice. I clicked them all closed, and I began to type my response to this ass, telling him exactly what I thought, how insulting, cruel, and pathetic he was, a grown man attacking a young girl because his entitled ass was not taken to a table of his liking. I told him emphatically to stay the hell away from my restaurant. I never wanted to see him again.

And so, it started.

From that moment on, I did not care. I had spent too many years reading ugly, offensive, lies about my restaurant and staff, and I could take no more. Sincere criticism is fair game, but you cannot lie or exaggerate—this is my business and my life. The public reads and believes. As these insolent reviews would appear, always marked with one-star, I began responding. I would let both the reviewer and the public know the truth, how their slanderous portrayal of events is not what really happened, and I was not, in any way, particularly nice about it.

Not at all.

The more insulting they were, they more insulting I was. Maybe it was the caffeine in my early morning coffee, maybe I worked too hard, or maybe I was just pissed that the world had come to this, but one thing was for sure—what I wrote was far from the nonconfrontational and apologetic guidelines for responding to customer reviews suggested by Yelp.

It was game on.

At first, my partner was horrified. He could not believe that I would write a response to a customer on Yelp and say they were crazy and tell them never to show their face in the restaurant again. Or that I questioned how anyone could believe some woman's criticism of my food since she was so drunk that night, I saw her falling off her heels on the way out. He was worried that potential customers were going to read this stuff, think that I was impertinent, and stay clear of restaurant. And to be honest, I was kind of scared, as well.

But you know, some things you just have to do.

And boy, did my responses get under the skin of these self-righteous posters. They were aghast and appalled that I challenged them, that I had not reacted subserviently as did other business owners with those hosts of gooey sweet apologies but instead called them out on their insolence. They frequently reposted even more slander, calling me every name you can imagine, though I did not play the back-and-forth game — my one response proudly stood firm. I always figured if they didn't want to hear what I thought about them, then they should have behaved better.

Initially, my biggest fans of these droll responses were my servers, the poor punching bags who bear the brunt of disgruntled customers. They knew I had their backs. They would alert management immediately of an impending issue and we would all try so hard to prevent problems. But sometimes, it was to no avail. We knew a review was brewing, that instead of someone just enjoying an evening out, they obsessed about getting home to post their wrath. Once I even remember a lady who sat pissed off at a table across from her complacent husband with an empty plate of food in front of her, typing a bad review on her phone. She was in plain view for all to see her.

As more time passed, I noticed that an unlikely fan base was developing. People would ask to meet me. They wanted to see the guy who wrote that stuff. I would hear, "Oh my God, we love you. . . . We love that you tell these people to fuck off. . . We laid in bed crying with laughter last night. It's the funniest shit we've ever read."

I would just stand there.

What was going on?

Why were people reacting like this? I would hear this stuff all the time. People would tell me the only reason they came to the restaurant was to meet me. I had other business owners stand at the table to shake my hand.

After a while, I began saving some of these reviews left by dysfunctional customers along with my accompanying, snarky replies. To demonstrate to you just how horrible some people can be and how all they want is to slander your business and for you to fail, I will share just a few of the posts and, of course, my humble responses.

Please know I have not deleted or changed a word. They are presented in their entirety as they were originally posted on Yelp. I even kept the posters' real names in hopes that one of these misfits reads this and realizes that what they wrote has been included in this disgraceful lot.

Susan O.

Van Nuys, CA

Why isn't there a zero-star option? We've had a reservation here for over a week and they just now canceled 3 hours before the reservation due to the chance of rain. Inexcusable. Why make a reservation when you can't keep it? That might lead to less of chance of leaving a group of four without any dinner reservations on a very busy evening.

Comment from Business Owner

Your reservation was specifically for the patio. Next time, you're welcome to come and sit in the rain. We'd be happy to serve you there.

Brandon H.

Santa Monica, CA

This is a terrible restaurant. I went in there by myself and they made me feel awkward because I was there to eat by myself. Then they brought me to the outdoor seating, and they made it seem like there was nowhere for me to sit because I was only one person. There were several tables available. There were 3 different staff there when this happened. I was told by one of the staff, "I guess I could sit at this table, but you'll be sitting here all by yourself." I walked out. Bad establishment!

Comment from Business Owner

There was nowhere for you to sit when you arrived because we were really busy and were saving tables for people who, unlike you, MADE RESERVATIONS. It had nothing to do with that fact that you were by yourself, you jerk. My manager tried to make you happy, but you walked out after a hissy fit, went to another restaurant, and sat there alone to type this review on Yelp. You're a mess, dude.

Samantha R.
San Diego, CA

Third time is not a charm. Arrived for our 8:15pm reservation, were told our table wasn't ready and handed a buzzer with instructions to wait at the bar. No apology or indication as to how long the wait time would be. After 30 mins we were seated. My drink order was forgotten and had to be repeated, again with no apology. Waited over 45 mins for the mains to arrive after our appetizers had been cleared away. Still no explanations or apologies even when we asked how much longer we had to wait. Portion sizes were large again but felt it was not worth the money or the wait. Have been here twice before and this was definitely the most disappointing.

Comment from Business Owner

I love technology. Our system time stamps everything. You arrived at 8:20 for an 8:15 reservation. You
were seated at 8:39, that's 19 minutes of a wait, not 30.
According to the kitchen ticket, you ordered entrées at
8:55, which cooked for about 25 minutes. So, you didn't
wait 45 minutes. You left at 9:55, 35 minutes after you
were served entrées. That's 1 1/2 hours total dining time
for a party of 4 on a busy Friday night. What motivates
someone to write something like this with all the exaggerations and what's up with all the apologies you seem
to require? What's wrong with you?

John H.
Palm Desert, CA

*On our visit last week, one incident there left us disap-
pointed in what otherwise should have been a wonderful
time. It was a birthday celebration, and we brought our
own wine. Our friend announced to the server that she
had a Wine Vault card, took the card out of her purse and
placed it in the middle of the table in front of the server.
The Wine Vault card is accepted by many of the best
restaurants around and allows the member diner's group
free corkage. When the bill arrived, we were surprised
to discover that NO corkage fees had been removed. We*

RUNNING THROUGH THE SWINGING DOORS

spoke with the server and the manager and they told us they didn't accept the card and we would have to pay the corkage fees. This was inappropriate given that we presented the card to the server when we arrived, and he said nothing at that time. If he had told us they would not honor the card when we presented it, we would have certainly taken the second bottle home and not ordered dessert. Then we would not have incurred the $50 corkage, dessert charge, which we wouldn't have ordered, and the additional tax and tip. The restaurant erred in being intransigent in light of the server's action and left us annoyed and disappointed.

Comment from Business Owner

Here's what really happened. Your friend laid some card on the table and never said a word to the server that you hoped not to pay corkage for bottles of wine you brought from home. No one saw your card. You drank your wine in our restaurant and then complained rudely and with persistence to the staff that you were a member of some club and wanted the charges waived. Next time you want to bring wine to a restaurant, ask them first at the front desk what their policy is and whether they participate in your club. And you told the server that the only reason you ordered dessert was because you thought you were saving money on corkage and additional tip? Really? You know, you could have saved even more money if you would have eaten dinner and drank your wine at home.

Amanda T.
Orange, CA

This place is beautiful. I've enjoyed the paradise-like patio for years. Recently, our group of 13 experienced extremely poor service and a few issues. We addressed the manager, and were promptly made aware that our concerns and the integrity of their customer's experience; we were disregarded... My colleagues and I felt poorly treated. Unanimously. The obscurity of customer service may have been a unique inconsistency for a restaurant that I enjoy. However, the owner's comments to any poor yelp review makes me want to never be a customer at his establishments. If I have a bad experience because then I am obviously stupid, a liar, a poor chef, have no life, an exaggerator or an idiot. While sometimes I am all of these, I do not want to be made aware of that when I am paying you.

Comment from Business Owner

OK Amanda, here's the story. For the past 8 years, I've worked about 70 hours a week in my restaurant. I have about 80 employees, all of whom try their very best to serve you, or they wouldn't be there. Anyone in customer service knows that a portion of the public will say anything or lie to make a point, especially if they can hide behind an anonymous blog like Yelp. Everything I write on this site is true. But people like you think that business owners should fall to their knees to make you happy. Sorry, that's not me. We made a sincere attempt to appease your party that night but several of you found it necessary to band together and denounce my business. Guess that's fair since my staff all commented on what horrible guests you were that night as well. Lastly, I can't believe you spent the time to copy and paste so many of my past comments in your review—I'm kind of flattered. Makes me happy you read them all. Maybe now you'll chill the hell out when you're in someone else's restaurant as they try their best to appease your self-righteous ass. Copy and paste that.

Matt C.
Sacramento, CA
I went with a group and we ordered beer and wine during happy hour. The regular beers were half the price of my nonalcoholic beer which was $6.00 a bottle and barely cold and it took over five more minutes to get a cold glass. The happy hour sliders were cold when delivered and 20 minutes passed before they got them picked up. When they got back to us they appeared to have been

nuked. I happened to discuss this with a person who
knows they are behind in paying their suppliers!!

Comment from Business Owner
People like you shouldn't be allowed in restaurants.
Your review is filled with lies. Lie #1—you ordered an
imported beer that was $2 more than domestic. Lie
#2—we don't have a microwave in the kitchen. Lie
#3—we are net 7-days and current with every sup-
plier we have. But this is *not* a lie—you're 86'd from
the restaurant.

Jessica H.
Fullerton, CA.
We had a reservation. We had to wait over an hour and a
half to order our food! Food took about another 45 mins.
Food was good. Service was terrible. Orders were wrong.
The bussers were better than the actual server. Our server
was rude and made us feel like we were bothering him.
Sad to say I will never come back. Ever.

Comment from Business Owner
No one in the history of the restaurant waited an
hour and a half to order food. If you really sat there
and waited that long for a server to show up, then
you're an idiot.

Jennifer R.
Los Angeles, CA

HORRIBLE SERVICE!!!! We went for a bachelor-ette week and decided to eat here for dinner one night. Terrible mistake that ruined our trip. Our server was David was completely incompetent as a server. After taking our order, he did not stop by the table again without coercion. When the bride received her salad, it came with no dressing so we tried waiting for David to come back to notify him. Too much time passed so we needed to grab the busboy to find David. When we wanted to order more food, again needed to find the server. When we needed to pay, we needed to find the server to give him the payment. He never apologized for the inconvenience. Once we received out payment back, I was $10 short. We then asked for the manager to resolve the issue and to complain about the service we received. NOT ONCE did she apologize for the server or for the miscount of money back. She never offered any compensation, only excuses for the server and to tell the owner. As we were walking out, we overheard the manager talking about us to other employees. SO UNPROFESSIONAL! No one apologized, no one tried fixing the problem, nothing was done.

Comment from Business Owner

Yes, we were talking about your table when you left because none of us could believe how bazaar you all were. It was 10PM on a Sunday night and we put it off to you being tired, or partied-out, or high. The salad was lightly dressed, as ordered, and when David offered to get more dressing, your friend was actually *crying*. It's not normal to cry for more salad dressing in a restaurant, sorry. David is an awesome server and said he was often at your table. You even gave him a 20% tip so he couldn't have been that bad. Anyone coming to dine with us should request him and I will absolutely defend him and his table service to a group of rude, creepy bachelorettes.

Linda V.
San Diego, CA
Food came out way too fast to have been prepared for us. They make all of this stuff ahead of time. Food was cold and quality you could taste was just not great. Place is probably ok for drinks, but I would avoid eating here again.

Comment from Business Owner

Yeah, you caught us, Linda. We pre-make all the food at the beginning of the night and leave it just under heat lights, hoping that someone will order it. You ordered a Pupu platter which consists of many small little items on a plate. The hot items go from the grill to the plate to your table. After two minutes on your table, the chicken satay is now room temperature. But you had to have a little strip of chicken on a stick steamy hot in order to eat it, so we re-heated everything for you because you're neurotic. I bet everything in your world is too hot, too cold, too fast, or too slow—never just right. Plus, you were out of the restaurant just 15 minutes and you had to sit with your cell phone to post this review. Why don't you just chill and enjoy your weekend in town instead of having to warn the public that someone should "avoid eating here"? The public will be fine without your warning.

James R.
Los Angeles, CA
Did anyone else get sick last night? Three in our group have terrible food poisoning. It was definitely the restaurant; we didn't eat anywhere else that night. It came on in the morning, 12 hours later and we drove home with multiple stops thanks to your food.

Comment from Business Owner
It amazes me how we can serve literally thousands of people in a weekend and when someone gets sick,

right away it's the restaurant's fault. Well, only your table got sick. Interesting how all of your other reviews are either 1 or 2 stars and you even claim to have gotten sick from food somewhere else. Maybe you should cook at home. Then you can blame yourself.

John V.
Palm Springs, CA

Dinner was good but at the end, they should have brought out the birthday cakes so that the birthday people could have seen them and lit the candles that we brought so we could have sung happy birthday to me. They cut the cakes and brought out pieces without even clearing the table!!! No one saw the decorated cakes! We complained to the server, asked to see the owner (we saw that the owner was there) but they just sent out some other guy that said the owner won't see us and said that it's too bad but we're getting charged anyway. Their attitude really sucks. This isn't the first time we've had a bad experience there and they refused to take care of it. We've always loved the ambiance there, but we will never go back. $600 bucks, waisted.

Comment from Business Owner

You are a tragic mess. I could write forever about your review, including the fact that your grammar sucks.

For the record, as some of your guests were leaving the restaurant, they rolled their eyes at your behavior and apologized on your behalf. First of all, we always tell guests there's a cake presentation fee to avoid cheap asses like you from complaining they were never told—the maître d' did not make a big deal about this—you did. Regarding your cake, the server desperately tried to light candles to sing to your pompous ass, but they kept blowing out in the wind and the 20 guests at your table were loud, drunk, and could care less about your birthday cake. Anyway, it was brought to my attention, but I was having dinner myself with family and the last thing I was going to do is listen to your trauma at the host stand about how your birthday weekend was ruined (as you said). You see, I would have told you, like I'm going to tell you now, that you're a big, spoiled baby. Just 20 feet over the wall from your patio table were homeless people sleeping on blankets on a hot, desert night and you are complaining that your weekend was ruined because your whole table didn't get to see your cake? Most of your other reviews on Yelp are 1-star and on the night of your birthday, you rushed home to type another. And for the record, we did not charge you for your cakes as you said, but we should have. I remember clearly who you are and better never see you again in my restaurant. Pathetic.

Debbie O.
Muenster, IN
No one liked their food. The Mahi-Mahi special was uncooked and disgusting. My husband's brisket burger was raw. My Ahi appetizer was so hard, I couldn't cut it. On and on. Then it was time for the bill and the pretty waitress said, "On parties over 6 we add a tip, would you like 20 percent? 22 percent or higher??" It was awkward, we had bad service and bad food, one person never had her water glass refilled all night. We had been there 3 times in the last month. It is now off our list.

Comment from Business Owner
Good job, Debbie—this is your very first review on Yelp and it's a 1-star? Superb. Whenever someone writes that absolutely everything a party of 6 people ate was horrible, including the service, then I am done. It is just not true. Not at this restaurant. Guess back in Munster, Indiana, where you come from things are done better. My favorite part of what you write is that we're off your list.

Meredith H.
Irvine, CA
Use to be favorite place to take friends and family, after our last experience of being pushed through our dinner by our server we won't be returning any time soon. Apparently turning tables is the priority not customers dining experience.

Comment from Business Owner
Whatever. Nothing's ever good enough. If your server had let you take your time, you'd complain he was inattentive. You would be surprised how effective a simple comment to your server such as, "We'd like to take our time" works. But it's all for the best—we'll have more room for others since "you won't be returning any time soon."

———————————

Paul M.
Indio, CA
We sat on the patio last night. Had three gusts of wind and sand. Table, tablecloth, menu, and drinks were all full of sand. No special accommodations were made. I would not suggest this place specially if it's windy. Specially if the meal was over $200.

Comment from Business Owner

You have got to be kidding. This just may be the dumbest thing I've ever read on this site. A wild desert storm hits, and you are complaining that during 70 mph gusts of wind and sand on an outdoor patio, your table got dirty? We couldn't get people off the patio fast enough – power lines were down – people could barely even walk outside – it was chaos. What sort of special accommodations would you suggest? An underground storm shelter so you could have dinner? C'mon, man.

So, there you have it. Just a taste of the social mania coughed up by this group of self-proclaimed Yelpers. This is not normal behavior. It is as though a segment of adult society never grew up and continue to act like toddlers in public situations, particularly restaurants. They think it is socially acceptable to yell, swear, threaten, and pound their fists on the host stand when they don't get what they want. I have had people verbally harass my hosts because they waited five minutes past a reservation time for a table, though in a doctor's office, a thirty-minute wait is typical, and at a concert, you can easily sit an hour before it begins. But I get it—you cannot make everyone happy. There is always someone who expected more, someone whose chicken is not quite hot enough, but c'mon dude—do you really have to get online as you walk out the front door and rip the place apart?

People like to pick on restaurants, and they are easy prey since the restaurant business is so competitive and so fragile. Restauranteurs will do just about anything to keep you around—and the group of toddlers is very well aware of this. So, they come, they demand, and they bully.

But let me tell you who are *not* toddlers—those who have worked in restaurants. No server who has ever stood tableside and borne a customer's offensive rant walks into another restaurant and raises hell or runs home after dinner to post a one-star review. And no kitchen cook would ever think of sending another cook's food back to the kitchen. No matter what. They eat and think about it but say nothing.

Nevertheless, as I read the plethora of online criticism with which I am now bestowed, I try to focus on normalcy, those who criticize with kind respect and appreciate people's work—the ones who, along with the bad, see the good, and the ones who have fun with friends, enjoy their time, are a pleasure to know, and who leave the restaurant at the end of their evening with a wave of their hand or a hug.

This keeps me smiling and keeps that cynical bastard that lives deep inside me at peace.

PRIVILEGE

*"Never argue with an idiot. They will only bring you down
to their level and beat you with experience."*

GEORGE CARLIN

For a nine-year period in the middle of my life,
I owned a beast of a large, commercial bakery.
Thousands of loaves of crusty boules were baked every
day, as well as scones, muffins, biscotti, and the like.
It ran around the clock and functioned with rotating
teams of bakers and packaging people. The aroma of
baking bread permeated a full city block near the bakery. My graveyard-shift bakers were tough men—they
worked from late at night until the sun came up, tossing
hundred-pound piles of dough from bench to bench,

dripping with sweat, smoking cigarettes to the filter, and put up with no shit. One morning when I arrived, my lead baker had just finished his shift and was leaving. As we stood outside on the sidewalk and chatted a minute, a Los Angeles police car drove by. My baker's head followed the car, then turned back to me, pulled the cigarette out of his mouth, dropped it to the pavement, and said in his French accent, "You know, those guys come into the bakery every night. They don't say a word—they just go into the refrigerators, grab bags of cookies and pastries, and walk out. It happens all time. Fucking guys."

That is called privilege. That is what this chapter is about.

Scattered throughout restaurants are certain individuals who feel they have special rights, whether it is a 7:30 p.m. reservation, a heavy pour on a glass of wine, or the best table in the house. Every restaurateur around can tell of customers who order an entrée, eat most of it, complain to the server that it was cold, salty, or overcooked, and then *insist* it be taken off the check. It has been the trigger to more confrontations than I care to remember. Why would someone think this is acceptable behavior? The answer is that they do not—they know it is wrong—but they just don't care. They know they can get away with it, and they know that restaurateurs willingly comply.

Over decades in this business, I have seen literally hundreds of people have temper tantrums in the dining room because they were not getting what they wanted. When there is an issue with someone's food, I usually just let them have their way since it is just so exhausting to hear their arguments and justifications for why they should not be charged. I have had customers sit at the table with their arms crossed pouting like a child for a half hour after everyone else at the table was gone because they did not like their dinner and wanted it removed from the check. I have even had customers stubbornly wait for police to arrive to resolve the conflict, thinking that justice would be served in their favor—but on the contrary, by law, you must pay for what you ordered, regardless, or you can be arrested. Ordering food in a restaurant is considered a legally binding verbal contract. But many people do not understand this. Instead, they think the rule is—if you do not really *like* it, you do not have to pay for it.

My rule is always very simple: If you eat it, you should pay for it.

Some people have absolutely no social grace. They will make a scene, demand to see a manager, raise hell, and not care about the other unfortunate people dining with them. Whenever I encounter one of these loud-mouths at the table, sitting there complaining about everything and sending the waitstaff into turmoil, it is quite obvious that the other people at the table are accustomed to these tantrums, as they just sit there, facedown and embarrassed, and often apologize to management when they leave on behalf of their bellowing friend.

This is not how it has always been. When I was a boy and was taken to a fancy restaurant, people did not behave like this. If you did not care for something, you would likely eat it anyway or leave it on the plate, then pay for it and probably not return. At some point in the 1980s, large corporate restaurants became so over-the-top accommodating that, regardless of the issue, the manager, with a grin plastered on his face, enthusiastically removed it from the check. No questions asked. Corporate leaders put forth policies that managers should appease guests at all costs. It was a numbers game, and the cost of voided food or alcohol just became another line item on a corporate expense report. It was non-personal. This is when we first started hearing that the customer was always right. Plus, these businesses had the support of obliging servers who always took the side of the irritated customer, since servers knew it would frequently land them more tip. And remember, all a server cares about is their tip. If a server had to pay for a customer's comped food, there would be a lot less comped food.

Hence, we are blessed with a flock of social misfits scattered among dining rooms of restaurants everywhere who think that a casual complaint is all it takes to get out of paying for dinner. It has nothing to do with how good it tastes or whether the steak is overcooked. But struggling restaurateurs in such a competitive business have become obsessed with doing whatever it takes to assure a guest returns. They just want people to leave happy, even if it means eating crow and taking a loss.

As is frequently the case, whenever a guest demands something removed from a check, it ultimately lands in my lap for resolution, and the scenario typically pans out in a similar way every time. First, almost psychically, information is whispered through the employee underground that the guy on table 83 is a problem.

The entire staff who is working in a restaurant always becomes aware of a disgruntled guest.

Then, as it goes, I receive a forewarning by the server as he runs by me. The server says, "As the busser cleared the guy's plate at table 83, the guy told the busser his chicken was too salty."

I find the busser and say, "Where's the chicken you cleared from 83?"

The busser says, "He ate it."

I say, "How much of it?"

Then they say, "Everything. There was nothing on the plate."

Okay. I have my facts. There is absolutely no reason why the busser wouldn't tell me the truth; he doesn't care. All he cares about is clearing the next table and filling someone's water glass.

When it's time to present the check, the server comes to me and asks what to do, whether we should comp this guy's chicken or leave it on the check. The server tells me he checked on the table several times and no one mentioned anything. At this point, I weigh my options—either I present the check and wait to see what happens, or I take it off the check and allow him to get away with it.

My decision is often based on several factors, such as how busy we may be, whether I need the table for another reservation, whether this guy is eating dinner with someone I know, whether he is a local customer or a tourist just passing through for a night (they are the worst), or if service is almost over after a hectic evening and in lieu of ending my night with an argument, I opt to let him have his way and I just sit down and have a glass of wine.

In my early years, I acted out of principal. I hated knowing that someone was taking advantage of my staff, my business, and me. I challenged them, something they were not expecting, and called them on their charade. They would yell at me and threaten, "I'll never be back," and I would answer, "Fine—pay your check and get out." These episodes sometimes escalated more than you could imagine.

As the years passed, I mellowed. My participation in these confrontations occurred less often, and I would generally opt to sit down and have that glass of wine. I began to see this sorry lot in a sad and sympathetic light. You know, when I would stand across the dining room and peer at them, I would often see a wrinkled unhappiness in their faces. They never smiled, and rarely looked like they were having fun. They were more concerned with the operation of the restaurant and how often the busboy filled their water glass than the good time their friends were having at the table. I began to accept it was not my purpose to fix them or teach them how to behave in public. God knows I tried. I realized everyone has their own lessons to learn.

The bigger the city, the more often these confrontations occur. In Los Angeles, when a guest had an issue, the first thing he always told me was what he did for a living—as though that made a difference or I really cared. Right off I hear that he is a vice president at Sony or that he works in the editorial department for the *Los Angeles Times*. As he enlightens me with his résumé, I think, *Oh God, here we go.*

Then it starts—he is appalled that his server never told him the four shots of Don Julio 1942 tequila he ordered were forty-five dollars each. Instead of the subservient response he expected from me, such as, "Oh my, let me speak with your server and see if there something I can do," I would say, "Well, why didn't you ask him how much they were before you ordered them since the price seems to be important to you?" Whenever I was straightforward and would say what I honestly felt, as sincerely as I could, it would be an issue. Confrontational guests in a restaurant expect management to bow down to them.

This scenario is a frequent riff at the bar. People order drinks, buying rounds for their friends and even for strangers, and are unaware about how much they are spending until they get the bill. To make matters worse, when it's time to pay, they are often drunk and there are few things more challenging than trying to rationally reason with a drunk person.

When I talk to someone who's had too much to drink, especially one who is annoyed, I know it's best to just let them talk. I pretend they're a child just having an outburst. I agree with everything they are saying, thank them for bringing it to my attention, tell them I will take care of it, and hopefully they walk away. Usually at this point, something distracts them, and they forget why they were just in my face. I learned this from years with bartenders. A good bartender has mastered this art. They regularly handle drunks—whether it's the guy who drinks half a bottle of bourbon or the bachelorette who drops to the floor after a strong margarita.

Drunk people fall into two basic categories—good

drunks and bad drunks, and any hopping bar has an equal share of both. The good drunks are difficult to spot. They laugh and have a good time, and it's only when the bartender sees how many drinks they have had that they realize it's time to cut them off. Good drunks frequently become alcoholics because they do not cause problems. Rarely is there need for intervention; they just keep drinking and having fun. Bad drunks take a different path.

A bad drunk is always the first person in the crowd who wants a drink. They buy the first round, and they want everyone to drink with them. They have fun, making toasts, laughing loud, buying shots, and just cannot drink enough. Then, in a moment, they change—the life of the party turns into your worst nightmare. All of a sudden, someone has to take care of them, and they become loud, angry, irrational, belligerent, and sloppy. This is when their friends say, "Oh shit, here we go." At this point, it becomes everyone's goal, both the bartender and their friends, to just get them out of the bar and hope they pass out in the backseat of a car.

Cutting off a guest who had too much to drink always, without exception, sucks, and no bartender or manager ever wants to do it. No one wants to hear they cannot buy another drink, especially someone who is drunk. Bartenders usually start by watering down the guy's next drink. They fill a glass with ice and water then float a bit of vodka on top. When he takes the first sip, he tastes vodka and is happy. In reality, it's a vodka-flavored glass of water.

If a guest must be cut off, it must transpire with discretion. He cannot be humiliated or embarrassed; it must be covert. It is best to whisper in his ear that he should probably call it a night and ask if he would like you to get him a cab. Another option is to coax the guy's friends into handling the situation—which they usually do by dragging him away. The goal is to get him or someone to pay for his drinks, to get him outside, and to make sure he does not drive.

Just another day at the office.

When it comes to expensive bottles of wine, the rules of the game change. The stakes become higher since a bottle of good wine costs a lot more than a cocktail. It does not happen often, but it certainly happens—a customer scans a wine list, he may recognize the names of a few wineries, but often, he does not. His wine choice is likely based on its catchy name, where it was produced, or the price. Wine-drinking protocol suggests the guest tries a bit in a glass to assure the wine is not "corked," or spoiled. But, every so often, usually from a place of ignorance, the snob dismissively shuns the wine, claiming it is not good—a pompous swirl in a glass, then a sip, followed by a sneer on their face and while shaking their head, they mutter, "Oh, no, no—this is not good. Can I see the list again?" The server thinks *fuck*, carries away the bottle, and finds the manager, or in most cases, me.

I remember years ago during a private wine tasting held at a prominent Napa vineyard, the sommelier, a man whose life was dedicated to producing and understanding fine wines, told me that these days, with sophisticated bottling machines and sanitation practices, *almost never* is a bottle of wine truly corked. He told me, statistically, it's about 1 in 100,000, and it mostly occurs in cheaper, mass-produced wines. "The good stuff," he said, "well, it never happens—it used to thirty years ago, but not anymore."

So, there I stand, with a returned ninety-five-dollar bottle of wine in my hand and a bewildered server staring at me for guidance. Sometimes, if I taste the wine at the table with the snob, I can sway him to keep it—but that is rare. Instead, I often get frustrated, roll my eyes, walk away, and just let the dude pick something else. The server would *always* tell me after, "Oh yeah, he liked that one much better."

Whatever.

So why do people return bottles of wine?

When it comes to wine, most people cannot tell the difference between a thirty-dollar bottle and a hundred-dollar bottle.

First of all, when a guest tastes wine, they usually do so right after they arrive at the restaurant, often before eating anything. The last thing they did before they got there was likely brush their teeth, use mouthwash, or have a mint before they picked up their date. Mouthwash and "three-hour" mints are designed to linger on your palate and can screw up the taste of anything. Plus, as any real wine pro knows, a high-end bottle of red has to open a while and be allowed to "breathe." This aerating process mellows the harshness of some wines and makes a marked difference in what you taste. What makes matters worse is that, most often, the wine is returned simply because they did not care for it, not that it was corked. It is returned because it is too dry, or sweet, or tannic, or even the wrong temperature. I remember once a guy ordered a red wine, sent it back, reordered a white wine, and as I walked away, I heard his wife say, "Yeah, I really wanted white wine tonight."

I drank a lot of remarkable returned wines with my dinner over the years.

———————————

The parade of the privileged march through restaurants in full force during holiday weekends or whenever more out-of-towners are around. Anonymity certainly makes it easier to pull off an insolent act—if they know they will not be seen again, then the burger is definitely overcooked, and it must be taken off the check. These people are very aware of the complacency that restaurant managers readily put forth—sure, no problem sir, we can adjust your check.

Now we come to millennials, that piteous group of young digital technology specialists and social media aficionados who have spent so much time staring down at their cell phones during their lives that they missed the lessons of social behavior, especially those pertaining to restaurants. No one more dismissively returns food to the kitchen with such nonchalance and indifference as do they.

Enter the bachelorettes—gaggles of celebratory young women who are out for a good time, often brash and aggressive, and in an uncanny reality, all seem to look alike. They can act as though it's a privilege that they have graced the restaurant and are right up in my face if more than five minutes passes beyond their reservation time, glaring at the host as they hold a sugary drink in one hand and a cell phone in the other. Once seated, their little celebration has the potential to turn into a service nightmare. Only my most seasoned servers, those well-versed in handling the nuances of such affairs, get the assignment since these young ladies could stretch us all to our limits.

Here is a typical scenario:

The group of young ladies are seated, all order dinner, and are served their entrées. Ten minutes later, one flags down the server and says, "You know, I'm going to have the salad that she's eating instead. Thank you," and points to her friend's salad.

"Is there something wrong with your pizza?" the server asks.

"No. I'd like that salad instead. Thanks!" And she turns away.

The server removes the pizza, returns to the kitchen, and tells me what happened. I look at her across the room and see someone sitting there whose hair, makeup, nails, shoes, clothing, and phone easily add up to a thousand dollars. I walk over to her and ask her what's wrong with the pizza she sent back. She seems appalled I would ask.

"Ah, I just don't want it. I'll take that salad instead."

"Okay, no problem," I say. "Since there was nothing wrong with the pizza, I'll box it up and you can take it home. Your salad will be right out."

She says nothing.

As I walk away, I notice her whispering to her friend. We serve her the salad, and she eats half of it. Later, when the group gets the check and sees both pizza and salad on it, she asks to see a manager and demands the pizza be removed.

After a few minutes of verbal boxing, the charade ends simply because, by this point, I am so tired of her, I just take it off the check so she leaves. As she walks out in her $150 heels, with the half-eaten pizza still in a box on the table, we make eye contact and glare at each other. Within minutes of her walking out the front door, I get an alert on my phone that she just posted a review on social media detailing what a horrible experience they all had, especially after they spent so much money at the restaurant. And she includes how rude I was, and as is always the case, that she would never be back. The review was all she had left to get even with me and prove to everyone that her behavior was valid, despite the reality. There is so little truth anymore in the popular culture.

Now I must end by stating this is certainly not the norm. By far, most of these bachelorette celebrations end with the group of ladies hugging the staff goodbye, giggling their way into the street. But so firmly planted in the psyche of restaurateurs is the desire to please that when we fall short, it demoralizes us. We remember the bad.

It is the tragedy of the day that replays in our mind as we lay in bed at night.

One could fairly reason that some of the public will naturally misbehave in restaurants—remember, there was always that one guy in school who was a troublemaker. It starts at an early age and is rooted in human nature, but what I couldn't foresee and still cannot believe is how much people steal. Hotels go to great extents to prevent guests from packing their suitcases with pillows, and towels, and hangers, or raping the mini bar for a shot of vodka or a Snickers bar—you can't check out of many places until your room is inspected by housekeeping and signed off. Well, to my naïve surprise, people even steal from restaurants, and you cannot prevent it. The semi-solution, I learned, was to buy cheap stuff that no one really wants. Salt and pepper shakers that you'd find at the dollar store lingered a lot longer than fancy ones, but without fail, bussers still come up to me and say, "We don't have enough shakers to set the tables." Everything disappears.

Other than customary contraband like shakers, napkin rings, sugar caddies, steak knives, bottles of Tabasco, etc., I have caught people ripping off more than you could imagine. One guy years ago had two full-sized table placemats—made of firm bamboo reeds as thick as pencils and that did not bend—stuffed under his shirt as he walked out of the restaurant. His shirt was stretched around the placements and it was ridiculously obvious what he was attempting to do. I looked at him and uttered with no hesitation, "What the hell are you doing?!" He grinned with embarrassment, pulled the placements out from under his shirt, laid them on the host stand, and walked out. Another dumbass.

Alcohol often fuels this pilfering since it hinders inhibition and encourages stupidity, but sadly, not everyone who takes stuff is drunk. Once, a young lady was actually trying to slip away with a lamp from the ladies' room—a cool, kitschy, Hawaiian-style fixture that sat on the counter. This wasn't an easy task, as she had to maneuver herself under the sink counter and re-weave the cord and plug back up through the pipes and countertop to free the lamp and then break it free from the glue that held it in place, but she did it, and she attempted the theft. With a crowd jammed at the front desk on a busy night, I saw her try to scamper past. I rushed over to her, grabbed the lamp, yanked it from her pasty hands, looked her in the eyes, and said, "Get out."

Interestingly, many people have actually stolen things and returned them the next day, obviously after they have lamented the crime and have sobered up. I kept a bronze business card holder at a host stand that taunted every impending thief that walked by. Twice I noticed it in the hands of rabble as they rushed out the front door, chasing them down the street to get it back, but eventually, one evening, it was gone. The next morning, sitting outside the front door was a small paper bag, stuffed with colored tissue, the bronze card-holder, and a note that said, "Sorry."

Everything must be glued down.

We designed and built a Tiki Lounge years ago in Los Angeles. It was a fabulous room with a thatched roof over the bar, rattan furniture, vintage artwork, strings of groovy-colored lights, and an amazing lava stone fireplace with a floor-to-ceiling Tiki god face and red-lit eyes. Throughout the years, I had collected really cool Tiki mugs, ceramic coconuts, like those they used in old Tiki bars such as Trader Vic's, the Beverly Hills' institution that had recently closed. I thought what a perfect idea it would be to feature these glasses and mugs for our rum-laden Tiki cocktails. So, I found a company that sold them and ordered many cases, about eight thousand dollars' worth. When they arrived, we unpacked and displayed them across the bamboo back-bar shelves, one more fun than the next—ceramic coconuts, mermaids, surfer dudes, Tiki men, and lava craters. When we opened, customers ordered these drinks as fast as we could make them, and the hip crowd would hang at the bar sipping from a straw in these cool tropical mugs.

Sure enough, you know what happens.

After a month, I noticed the back-bar shelves were about half full. I said to the bartender, "Where the hell are the rest of the Tiki mugs?" He said, "That's all we got. I think people are taking them." Yep, half were missing, and over the next couple of weeks, we had so few mugs that we couldn't make cocktails. I had given it a valiant effort, but I was done. I reordered plain, basic bar glassware that boringly sat on the shelves, and I kept the few remaining cool mugs for my private collection. Hundreds of mugs had been stolen. A server told me that one guy was actually pissed his coconut cocktail wasn't served in the usual ceramic coconut shell. The server told him, "Sorry, we don't use those anymore." The guy's smartass reply was, "Damn, I have seven. I wanted a set of eight."

Other than how much someone can stuff in their pocket or their purse, every restaurateur around has been victim to that group of social entitlement who walk a check without paying. It's hard to believe, but it happens, and when it does, it's always and most definitely a planned, intentional scam. Good servers learn the signs—one person heads to the restroom, then the other follows, or they both decide to go for a smoke at the same time. What a server looks for is keys or a cell phone left on the table—a sure sign they're returning, but when they take everything and head outside, you have to have your eyes open because, in a moment, they can disappear into the night.

With a bar packed full of happy-hour partakers one evening, I was alerted by a server that two young ladies sitting at bar table were getting pissy about an appetizer they had shared. He told me they each had four martinis and the one appetizer and were slurring words, and when presented with the bill, refused to pay for the appetizer, even though they ate it all. Eventually, they demanded to see the manager, and when I arrived at the table, before I said a single word, one yelled in my face,

"I'm not paying for it!" She was in her twenties and looked like she could have been attractive if she took care of herself. I stared her in the eyes and said, "You ate it." Then it started. For the next two minutes, she argued with me, and as her girlfriend recorded it all with her cell phone, she threatened me with bad social media reviews and began to curse. At that point, I said, "Okay, I'm done. Pay your bill and get out," and I walked away. From the other side of the room, I watched them just sitting there whispering to each other then, suddenly, like an alarm had sounded, they jumped up and ran into the parking lot. My reaction was primal, like a lion seeing a running antelope, and I started to chase after them. They sprinted out of the parking lot and into the streets, and for some strange reason, as though I was possessed, I just kept running after them. We were all running at full pace, around corners, over curbs, across streets, left and right, we just kept going. The whole time I was thinking about what I would do if they stopped and how it was going to end, then, by the grace of God, a police car just happened to turn the corner and see us. I yelled, "There! There!" pointing at them. He pulled his car over, got out, and now he was running after them. This was good, since it is never a smart move to run from a cop. Within moments, the ladies stopped, and with the last little bit of air in my lungs, I wheezed to the cop that they walked their check from my restaurant. The ladies started complaining about all the details, but he stopped them and said, "Look, I don't care about any of it. You pay your tab, or I take you to jail." Moments later, the policeman handed me her credit card, I jogged back to the restaurant, charged their bill, then went back with the card. I never saw or heard from them again.

Once, on a busy Saturday night many years ago, I had a group of eight adults come in for a table. Without a reservation, they waited a while at the bar, ordering martini after martini, apparently having a good time. When their table came up, they were seated, and the bar tab was transferred. Their party continued with more drinks and expensive wine and lots of steak entrees. No one thought anything of it—it's the kind of table a server loves—everyone was happy, and they were spending a lot of money. At one point, the server came into the kitchen and handed me a credit card.

He said, "Does this look right?"

I said, "Huh? This is made from cardboard. Where did you get it?"

"The eight-top gave me this to pay their tab?"

I said, "It's cardboard. It's a piece of cardboard printed with the American Express logo. C'mon—go get a real card!"

With that, the server left the kitchen—thirty seconds later, he returned, looked at me, and with the fear of God in his face said, "They're gone—no one's there."

In the time the server was sent on his diversion to the kitchen, this party of eight adults, on a hectic night, casually got up, said goodnight to the hosts, and walked out the front door. When we noticed they walked the check, the server, my managers, and I ran outside to find them. As I ran around the corner, I saw way down the street in front of me the group of eight running at full pace in the dark, and then they were out of site. Their tab was $1,200. Dinner was on me that night.

I had a friend years ago who ran an acclaimed New York restaurant who lost so much each year to theft, from both the public and his staff, that he actually had an expense line item on his P&L called *Theft*. Everything that was stolen or "missing" accrued in this category and he would expense it come tax time.

Most employee pilferage in restaurants occurs in the kitchen by cooks, and no matter how you try to control it, it goes on right in front of your face. I worked a brief cooking stint in a small diner in my twenties that was run by an arrogant owner who was not liked by any employee, the kind of guy who sat at his table during service and did nothing except shout out commands. At the end of service when everyone was gone, the dishwasher would mop the floors in the kitchen using the conventional yellow mop bucket on wheels. As he mopped the inside of the walk-in refrigerator, with the door closed, he'd load up the mop bucket with beef tenderloins, lamb racks, and assorted chops, all sealed tight in Cryovac plastic, submerging them in the dirty brown mop water. With the mop laid on top of the goods, he'd push the mop bucket back through the kitchen, out to the dining room, and right past the owner, who sat at his table, grinning and nodding to his faithful dishwasher. When the dishwasher got outside in the night, he'd dump the bucket of water and sealed meats in the bushes and later, in the middle of the night when everyone was gone, he'd return to collect his take. As I'd clean my station every night and as I watched the dishwasher push that bucket with the dirty mop, I always wondered what he had in the water.

Certain items you just cannot buy for cooks to use, like knives, since a new knife purchased for general use in a restaurant kitchen lasts only days, if that, before it bafflingly disappears. When you ask where the knife is, they all look you right in the eyes and say, "I don't know." But it's gone. Tongs, sharpeners, whisks, peelers, zesters, paring knives, strainers—all disappear and are constantly replaced. Cooks are also infamous for taking home uncooked dinner, such as a couple of steaks or a takeout container of raw shrimp that they later cook for their families, and try as you might, it cannot be controlled. At the end of the night, when they are left alone in the kitchen to clean up, things end up in their knife bags, backpacks, pockets, and purses. If questioned, it is all denied, and no one ever knows any-thing—the truth remains covert in the brotherhood of the cooks.

―――――――――――――――――

Displays of neurotic eating behavior are a frequent source of eye rolling and back-kitchen mockery among both servers and line cooks. How some people order food, or cocktails for that matter, can be almost embar-rassing. I never make a big deal of it, that maybe some guy wants a side of ranch dressing with his sushi—I fig-ure you're eating it, dude, whatever—but it certainly makes for amusing natter among the staff as we sit with our end-of-the-shift cocktails.

For example, there seems to be a slice of the popu-lation that prefers their food, and drinks for that mat-ter, separated. Not a night passes that someone doesn't order a vodka and soda with the vodka in one glass and the soda in another, though this is most likely their attempt to ensure an accurate pour of booze, cheap-skates that they may be. The fun begins when it starts with food—like a Cobb salad with the chicken on a side plate, the blue cheese on another plate, the bacon on another, the tomatoes on another, and of course, the dressing on the side—or the guy I remember who always insisted that no item on his plate should ever touch another item; he actually told the server that he wanted an *inch* between the meat, the potato, the vegetable, and the sauce. I swear to God.

I've had customers order chicken medium rare, or they ask for their steak to be simmered in water, instead of grilled, then cut up in tiny little pieces so they wouldn't have to cut it. Once, many years ago, a server advised me that a guy at his table wanted spaghetti tossed with ketchup, only ketchup. I thought it was a joke, but the server assured me the request was legit. I told the server I'd oblige, but no matter what, he had to pay for it. I made it, we served it, he ate it, and he liked it. I served whole, steamed artichokes one time with an aioli dipping sauce. After one customer was through eating, the server went over to the table and noticed there was absolutely nothing left on the plate. The server asked, "Ah, how was the artichoke?" The customer replied, "Oh it was wonderful. Parts were a bit tough but wonderful." There have been countless customers who've brought ingredients to the restaurant for the kitchen to prepare their dinner, or a homemade salad dressing, or a fancy cheese they wanted on a pizza. They ask for the bones to be cut off their chops, or the skin off a fish, or just the white rings of calamari—none of "those little, black, curly things." I made a brave attempt to serve grilled trout once with the head still majestically attached, as *every* restaurant in Europe does. After the third one was sent back to the kitchen to have the head removed, we removed them all.

You cannot teach people how or what to eat. You must give them what they want.

Apparently, people have developed allergies to just about everything, as any well-seasoned server can most certainly attest. I always instruct servers to ask a table when they're first greeted whether or he or she should be aware of any allergies. Someone always utters something like, "Oh yes, ah, I'm allergic to asparagus." Now, are they really allergic to asparagus? Have they had an allergy skin test where the little "asparagus" dot reacted as positive? Or could it be that perhaps they just don't *like* asparagus, or maybe they've never even tried asparagus.

Allergies are serious business, and to those unfortunate souls who live with them, it's an ongoing challenge to ensure their food is safely prepared. Peanut allergies are a perfect example. Some people are so sensitive to peanuts that it can be life threatening, their throat closing up just moments after contact. I had a woman come into the restaurant one busy evening and ask me if we could take four for dinner. I said, "Sure, we'll get you in here."

"Okay. Do you use peanuts in the restaurant?" she said.

"Yes."

"Oh, never mind then," she quickly responded.

"Why?" I said.

"My daughter has a severe peanut allergy. I won't bring her in here if you serve peanuts."

I assured this troubled woman that I was the chef, and that I would personally prepare her daughter's meal, promising her it would clean and peanut free. She sharply shook her head no, thanked me, and ran out the door. It was that bad.

Nonetheless, people proclaim "allergy, allergy" all the time—vegetables, garlic, Tabasco, gluten, MSG, pork, dairy, eggs, oils, and on and on. Once a woman told us she was highly allergic to *salt*, and the server boldly typed on the dinner ticket "severe salt allergy." Guess she didn't realize that everything in nature contains salt, including her body.

Then we come to those illustrious folks who want everything with the sauce on the side. It seems to me that this obsessive scenario is essentially a control issue, and those who order sauce on the side, SOS as we say, are controlling by nature. They are the one who made the reservation. They are the person at the table who directs everyone where to sit. They are the one who begins the conversation with the server first, who takes the longest to order, and they always finish with, "Better give me the sauce on the side." I've made study of people who order salad dressings SOS. When the salad is served, before the food runner even leaves the table, they dump the whole ramekin of dressing on the salad. It always happens, and frequently they ask for more. Why do people do this? If you're in a good restaurant, buzzing with people, you will most likely have a better experience if you just let the kitchen make the food as designed, but pretty much every ticket that comes up off the printer has some sort of a modification. No broccoli, sub asparagus. No blue cheese, sub goat cheese. No rice, extra veg. It's so common that the order entry systems are designed with lists of typical substitutions to make the order entry process faster for the servers. And for the record, it drives cooks nuts.

But any parent of a big family most certainly knows that some children just require a bit more attention than others. For them, you must explain more, take your time, assure them that they are okay, coddle, pamper, and hold their hand longer than the others. It's no different in restaurants. Some customers come in, eat, and go home. Others require much more love and consideration. These are the special ones.

LOCKDOWN

*"Hardships often prepare ordinary people
for an extraordinary destiny."*

C.S. LEWIS

Aside from vacations, I have not missed a Saturday night at work since I was a teenager. It's just part of the business, and anyone who works in a restaurant knows that hoping for a Saturday night off is an illusory dream. It is a nonnegotiable request—it's when restaurants are busy—the curtain goes up, it's show time. If you do not like to work weekends, then you should probably find another job. In my dad's restaurants, he used to joke he'd only hire homely girls since they would gladly work on Saturday nights.

One day comes along after all those Saturday nights that sets off what will be one of the most difficult periods I'll ever have. It changes everything for all of us for a very long time.

It is a typical St. Patrick's Day. There are bunches of green balloons decorating the bar, and the servers all have green beads hanging from their necks—we are looking forward to a busy night. Just as we get going, two Code Enforcement officers come in the front door of my Palm Springs restaurant and hand me an order stating that we must close for an unknown number of days due to the threat of a mysterious virus that had invaded America. This questionably written document from the mayor's office cites codes and section numbers that grants them the power to shut us down. We had never closed the restaurant, not even one night, in more than a decade, and it is now the middle of high season. We call around to other restaurants—they are complying. No one has any idea what this means, how long it would be, or if it's the end of the world. In a panic, we put a sign on the door, throw all the prepped food in the walk-in refrigerators, and go home.

The next morning, I ask a dozen of my cooks and prep people to come in to help me break down the kitchen. When I arrive at the restaurant, I walk into a group of somber, sad, and worried people just standing there, silent, looking at me for guidance and direction.

Where do you begin?

Most people have no idea what goes on in a high-volume restaurant kitchen with a complex menu that is open every day. There are a hundred sauces, dressings, and condiments that are kept ready to go at all times. When we need more of something, it is prepared, labeled, and stored in refrigeration. Meats and poultry are ordered daily and stored in sealed plastic packaging until it's marinated, refrigerated, then transferred to cook stations ready for when we get an order. Just the amount of fried chicken we have on hand is astonishing. There are dozens of cases in refrigeration, then a hundred pounds more in a marinade, then many sheet pans that had been floured ready to be fried to order, and this rotation continues day after day.

All of the cooks' stations are filled with *mise en place*, the many ingredients they use to make a dish. Large containers of iced-down fish line the walk-in and are heaped with shrimp, squid, salmon, tuna, and whatever else we may be selling, as well as dozens of pans of bread, pizza dough, desserts, and on and on.

Such is the life in a high-volume kitchen, and it takes many days to build an inventory of everything necessary to pull off a night of feeding hundreds of guests from a huge menu. It is a feat of organization and balance that takes a lot of time to develop.

A restaurant kitchen is an ecosystem—if one part fails, then it all fails.

So, there we stand, with orders to destroy it all. We begin packing our limited freezer space with as much as we can. We start pulling everything out of our two large walk-in refrigerators, saving things that would last, such as pickles or some salad dressings, and packing up a lot of things that could be taken home and used by employees like marinated meats, vegetables, and lettuces. Much is unsalvageable or not the kind of thing you would take home, like gallons of curry sauce, or buckets of cooked pasta we use when we make mac & cheese, or trays of pizza dough balls, or expensive orchids that garnish our plates. It is all thrown away.

As I watch my diligent crew of Latinos hustling and working, breaking down everything they worked to create, taking out garbage cans of unusable food ingredients, focused, quiet, looking at me for direction every minute, I have to pause two times to leave the kitchen so I can tear up alone in the men's room. It is just overwhelming. Something about throwing food away, even a sauce, is unnerving for a chef, especially me.

After six hours, we are finished. When I notice people standing around with nothing to do, I begin to send them home. As they gather up the food they are taking, one by one, each comes up to me, hugs me, and tells me in Spanish to call them when it is time to work again.

Shortly after, as I stand alone in the kitchen, I think about why we had to do this.

Who would have thought that someone getting a flu in China would break us all down? That all my employees, both in the kitchen and in the front of the restaurant, would look at me, worried, stressed, and wonder when they would make money again. Many live check to check, and that just may be the worst part—to know they may not make rent in a couple of weeks. I understand why we have to do this, but it is just so devastating for so many.

As I stand there, I think about the day that I could call everyone and say, "Let's go, it's time. We're opening!" And I smile.

Several days later, I find myself sitting quietly at home. I have a cocktail in my hand and realize, "Oh, shit, it's Saturday night."

So, this is what it's like?

Strangely, it seems like any other night, though I know that my normal is typically a frenetic chaos. I settle into the sofa and sip my glass.

As the days pass, every morning I head to the restaurant kitchen, where I go through the refrigerators, giving or throwing away vegetables, lettuce, dairy, little by little, as they became unusable, always in hopes that tomorrow we could open and I'd need them for service. But that day didn't come.

Fast forward five weeks of lockdown.

During that time at home, I cleaned, I organized, I bonded with my pets, I overdosed on cable news, exercised, and ardently tried not to gain weight. I found myself baking cookies in the middle of the afternoon, just for the hell of it. I canned pickles, made intricate Indian curries for dinner, and experimented with a gelato maker I once received as a gift. Every day at 5:00 p.m., my partner and I had cocktail hour—we would turn off our cell phones and all the virus updates that continuously spewed from the TV and would sit quietly outside and talk. The experience of having no responsibility was new to me and truly enlightening.

I don't think ever before in my life, I had nothing to do for such a long time.

Though, enjoy this as I did, the whole time a petulant little voice kept whispering in my ear, "Ah, remember . . . you have no income."

Ugh. Reality.

After a few more weeks, I begin to receive texts and phone calls from my Latino cooks, who humbly ask for financial help, most of whom are not on any government assistance. I meet them at the restaurant office and give them advances from our savings account, and they tell me how they were literally eating beans and rice, like when they used to live in Mexico. They seem different to me, relaxed yet stressed, wrapped in face masks, usually with several of their children in tow, whom I had never met. Though I had worked with many of them for years, it's fun to see the personal side of their lives and how their children look like little versions of them. Most of the kitchen crew had been accustomed to working days and nights, and they tell me about the challenges of living in small apartments with children out of school. They take their checks, along with an armful of produce from the refrigerators, ask me how much longer I think this lockdown will continue, and go on their way.

As more weeks pass and I realize that the likelihood of reopening our twelve-year-old restaurant is still very uncertain, I decide to try a takeout-only menu and bring life back to the quiet kitchen. Restaurants typically run with small margins, spending money to pay bills as soon as they get it. My savings account is being depleted more and more every day, as I still send out checks for utilities, rent, property insurance, health insurance, and other expenses—I need income.

The day before I fire things up, *after two months*, I walk through the peaceful facility. There is no hum of equipment, no smell of food, no people, no energy, no spirit. Nothing is quite as ominous as a closed restaurant. When they are busy, there's always someone around doing something, fixing equipment, receiving deliveries, making stock, or roasting peppers. But shutdown, it is as though you are standing in a dark, eerie graveyard, you and the energy of life that used to be.

It is like walking through the empty house of a relative who has just passed away.

So, one by one, I plug in refrigerators, turn on ice machines, organize the mats on the floor, relight pilots, and post a schedule of the skeleton crew that would arrive the next day to begin pulling it all together. I am so excited to make those calls with the good news. All of them answer their phones on the first ring with anticipation, like they have been just sitting there, waiting. Some scream, some thank God, one starts crying, and they all quickly answer me in Spanish, *"Si, si, cuando, cuando?!"*

The next morning, one by one, the cooks arrive with big smiles, thankful to work, chubbier than before, and instead of their typical shaved heads, they all have shaggy hair. It is awkward at first—we want to give bear hugs but laugh it off and instead do fist-bumps, still fearful that we might catch something. They head into the kitchen, a place where they had spent countless hours over many years, their knives in one hand, and backup masks in the other, greet their cooking coworkers, and go to their stations to sniff things out, like dogs coming home after a long trip away. They look around, rearrange things, settle in, and we push through the food prep list. They seem at home and very, very happy.

Two days later, the moment has arrived. Before the

first takeout order comes in, I have a brief meeting with the whole staff and attempt to explain how it would all work. Orders will be placed for pickup or delivery at specific times, be prepared, packaged, and set aside, ready to go. Business as usual, right? Not exactly. Our typical system of managing hundreds of guests is totally altered, and the evening quickly turns into that ill-reputed opening-night-of-a-restaurant scenario, everyone running, yelling, sweating, and anxiously trying to manage orders and uphold our reputation, which has taken us years to earn.

When it all ends, we are beat up, as though we have just finished a great cooking race and lost. We talk about how to fix the system for the next night, clean up, and quietly go home. As I drive, I think how blessed I am to have such an amazing group of employees around me, because I know, absolutely know, that the next night will be perfect. For me, and for many restaurateurs, staff is family.

It feels so good to be back with my family again.

After a few more weeks of serving only takeout with a limited staff and limited income, the effects of this great shutdown are becoming critical. I have seen my team of eighty suffer the loss of their jobs; most received no unemployment and still regularly asked to borrow money from me. The restaurant is barely breaking even. Everyone's stress level is off the charts.

One night, as we sit and wait for the phone to ring, two code enforcement officers from the City of Palm Springs walk in the back door. They are dressed like police and each wear sophisticated masks on their faces, as though they are heading into surgery. I can only see their eyes. One looks at me, says nothing, and points to his badge.

I say, "Can I help you? What's wrong?"

He responds like a computer and says, "A state of health emergency has been issued and mandates the closure of dine-in restaurants (like I didn't know that). You are in violation."

Across the outdoor patio at a distant table sits my office manager, who just got off work, with his wife and two-year-old. He ordered a takeout dinner and asked me if they could sit there and eat. I told him yes and there they sat, the three of them, eating out of plastic to-go containers. As you might guess, things escalate with these officers, who are demanding to see my business license. At one point, one pulls out his cell phone and walks away. In a panic, my manager and his family gather up their containers and leave. A minute later, two *real* police officers show up. Two others stay outside. Now six men and three police vehicles are parked outside.

As it turns out, one of the real police officers is sympathetic and actually apologetic. He convinces me to accept this bogus violation and fight it later. One of the code enforcement officers returns and lays a slip on the bar, like a spiteful meter maid putting a ticket on a car. He looks at me and says, "Read the back," and walks out. After everyone is gone, I read the citation. The fine amounts were lined-out by this guy and increased from hundreds of dollars to thousands. He gave me no warning, no understanding, no compassion, and couldn't care less that it was my employee who was eating there; he was arrogant and condescending.

Is this what the world has become?

I am handed a bogus ticket for a thousand dollars and have done nothing wrong. My first thought is never to pay the ticket—never. Fuck them. Instead, I'll use the money for more loans to my staff, who don't sleep because they're worrying about paying rent, while city officials sit at their microphones during council meetings and discuss the likelihood of another person catching something or whether they would permit businesses to reopen. Memorial Day is the next weekend and is usually the busiest of the year. We always beat the previous year's record—but not this year.

When I get home that night, I write about what had happened, post it on social media, and go to bed.

The next morning, a movement has begun. The post went viral and was being shared to hundreds of other websites by a thousand people. The public's outrage is obvious by the countless comments and messages that are posted and sent to me. News media contacts me for interviews. Lawyers offer me free council. The city's mailboxes are full of irate messages from citizens who are not only intolerant of such behavior but are absolutely sick of the stay-at-home lockdown. Many people even volunteer to pay the fine. One elderly couple from Texas actually sent me a check for twenty-five dollars to contribute to the cause. People have had enough.

That evening on the local news, the top story headlines the episode and includes comments from city officials. They announce publicly that they would cancel the thousand-dollar citation and would "look into" the incident. The next afternoon, after a council meeting, a customer tells us it is suddenly decided that restaurants can reopen. We waited for more than two and a half months for this news, and it comes to us with no advance notice, no official announcement, and no forewarning.

Well, I'll be damned if I'm not going to reopen!

Restaurant people know how to kick ass and rally when they need to.

We have the green light—we're opening. My managers grab phones to round up staff. "We're opening!" I can hear them yell. I desperately search the internet to find what conditions and restrictions are being imposed but find nothing.

An hour later, I receive an email from the county health organization that lists pages of mandates to be followed. Almost the entire document is dedicated to sanitation—how tables and chairs have to be wiped down after every seating; how bathrooms have to be cleaned; how menus are to be handled; and so on. Most of this is normal practice anyway, but new restrictions are put in place regarding table distancing, bar service, and a required mask policy for all employees.

The chaos over the next two hours is typical of any opening night. Dozens of people are running around trying to get organized. We are rearranging tables, filling spray bottles with sanitizing liquid, removing silverware from tables and rolling it in napkins, printing notices to be posted all over the restaurant, installing hand-sanitizing stations, and desperately calling vendors to see if we could get food deliveries. Cooks are asking me how much to prep and how many people will show up. I have no idea. We have to print a special limited menu since we certainly do not have everything ready. All lines on the phones are ringing with questions.

"Is it true?"

"Can we make a reservation for four?"

The public is as tired of staying home as we are.

It's Friday night of Memorial Day weekend, the busiest of the year. We adjust the lights, turn on the music, and unlock the front door.

We are open!

Guests arrive and slowly walk into the restaurant, as though they're cautiously stepping from a spaceship that just landed on another planet. People amble around with trepidation and look for guidance. We had all endured an historic, great isolation and it just ended. There are many teary-eyed friends who are making awkward approaches to hug and, upon realizing what they're doing, pull back with an uneasy chuckle. Everyone is relearning social behavior and, frankly, it sucks.

After an hour or two, our usual high-paced energy is beginning to return. Though we are only moderately busy, it seems so much more difficult than usual. Service is challenging and complicated with new sanitation procedures, bags of takeout orders, confused costumers, and a diligent staff fussing with uncomfortable masks trying to remember how we do things. It is opening night again, and we are rusty.

However, something odd is in the air.

I sense a feeling of peace among the staff and the clientele. It's like everyone is high, in some trippy, nirvana state of bliss. We are all so joyful and calm, just smiling as we pass each other, humbled to be liberated from the great lockdown, like a cancer patient who beats the disease and walks out of the hospital into sunshine. We did what they told us, we made it, and we are back. The restaurant quickly becomes as busy as ever, there's a party every night at the bar, and happy days are here again.

But the party only lasts two weeks.

Once again, a customer calls the restaurant, and to our surprise says, "I heard that you can't serve inside the restaurant anymore, only on patios, and bars must now be completely closed."

Sure enough, we're shut down again, this time the inside dining rooms, and all bar seating, with the deceptive promise that it would last only three weeks—yes, the "official" announcement from the State is *only* three weeks. Only? Three weeks is a death sentence for many restaurants who have already been closed for months, spent a lot of money on inventory and labor to reopen, and are now ordered closed again. Many restaurants do not have outdoor seating and are again crippled, plus places like mine that feature a bustling bar have to turn away a crowd that took years to build.

The promised three-week period flies by with no notifications from anyone, and desperate diners are forced to sit in the inferno of my outside patio. It is the beginning of August, when average *evening* temperatures are well over 100 degrees, and it's the onset of the dreadful "monsoonal" season of Palm Springs, when hot, humid air billows in from the south, making conditions as sultry as a Brazilian rainforest. Some nights, you can actually see the hot steam in the air and customers' clothing and hairlines are dripping with sweat as they quickly eat their dinners and run to air-conditioning. My servers suffer the most since they slog for hours in the steam house with masks fixed to their faces. At times, I tell them to resuscitate in the large, walk-in refrigerators, taking a few deep breaths to come to life again, and then head back out into hell to take someone's dinner order.

Making matters worse is the gut-wrenching anxiety that some customers are trying to overcome as they walk in the restaurant. I can see profound fear in their faces, like a doctor is telling them they have a terminal illness. Every night, someone confides in me, "This is the first night I've been out since March." It's been more than five months, and seeing other people walking around, having dinner near them, mask or no mask, is just too much for them. Many come in, tell me they can't handle it, and walk out. Often, there are confrontations, someone shouting at another who walks by without a mask, or someone coming up to me demanding I tell another to put on a mask. Some come in the front door and say, "Oh, do I need a mask?" Others simply refuse to wear one. Many take to social media to bash my business for serving too many people, though we adhere to the guidelines and have routine inspections from code enforcement teams. It's just a horrible, horrible time, and the evenings are layered with numerous challenges that are atypical to the restaurant business. Serving great food with great service becomes the easy part.

More than two months go beyond the promised three-week temporary closure. Those like me who manage to survive the lockdown are forced to set up dining tables anywhere they can as long as it's outside— in parking lots, on street corners, on sidewalks—and spend money they don't have to purchase umbrellas, lighting, music speakers, and outdoor furniture in vain attempts to make such uninviting areas more appealing to guests. For many restaurants, these attempts prove futile as guests scoff at the idea of having dinner on a hot, busy sidewalk alongside zooming traffic and exhaust. One day, after the release of a contrived method of determining how and when restaurants may operate, we are again permitted to seat a small percentage of the dining room, but still not the bar, and it comes with more assurances that slowly, over an indefinite number of weeks, or perhaps months, we will be able to return to full capacity and resume "normal" operations. Sadly, for many, it is too little, and too late, and countless restaurants—many of which have been around for decades, after years of hard work and dreams—and all their employees fall victim to the threat of some mysterious virus and the fear of the unknown.

Months seem to pass like weeks, and I begin to question what the real threat to our businesses might be. Rules change in a flash, and the line of communication to businesses seems to come from erratic posts on social media—close inside dining, only outdoors, then only small parties allowed outdoors, then limit the hours of operation, then a few weeks later, close all restaurant service, only takeout is permitted again, then outdoor dining is permitted again. Every morning, we'd all wake up and wonder what rules we'd have to follow that day. These surprises play havoc with the operation and not only cause enormous waste and financial turmoil for me, but devastate my staff, who live paycheck to paycheck, desperate to work, trying to budget income that is always fluctuating, and who spend each moment hoping that good things will soon happen, that the sun will shine again.

With the prosperous holiday season excitedly approaching, and as the restaurant runs with only a small part of the dining room available to seat, just days before Thanksgiving we are given dreadful news once again—we must close *all* table service and only takeout may be offered. Hundreds of reservations are cancelled and we pack our freezers with food we cannot sell. This time, rumors fly that the shutdown may last months, well into the next year, and as the days tick by, one by one, we tune in for weekly updates from the state governor, who always seems to paint a grim and disparaging picture—at all costs, the public must stay home. Serving takeout-only food doesn't even come close to paying the bills piled high on my desk. About 90 percent of the staff is unemployed again, and I'm inundated with daily requests from many of them to borrow money. The two weeks that surround Christmas and New Year's, always the busiest time of the year, are simply passed by, and we are all left feeling frustration, anger, and hopelessness. Many of my fellow restaurateurs and I form an underground society and speak of defying the ordinance and just reopening, but threats circulate of severe fines and penalties that would be imposed if we do so. With little survival time left, after two long, depressing months, and with no notice, one early morning, I see a post on Facebook from the *Los Angeles Times* announcing that restaurants may once again reopen for *outdoor* dining.

Am I supposed to be happy?

Am I supposed to be happy that the governor of the state where I've worked for forty years has decided over the weekend that conditions have so drastically improved since his dismal analysis just one week prior that we could now reopen our restaurants? Am I supposed to believe that his directives that critically affected so many lives had basis in facts, especially since the data was never made public? Am I supposed to be happy that we could now run our restaurants for outside dining only, ignoring the reality that many of my fellow restaurateurs have no patio, but instead must try to line their sidewalks and parking lots with tables on chilly, winter nights, as dining rooms remain empty? Am I supposed to be happy that my business will once again be subject to that contrived colored tier system that determines how many more weeks, or maybe months, must past before I can sit someone at a booth inside? Are my employees supposed to be excited to work again now that their savings has been completely spent, they've run up debt, are behind in rent, delinquent on payments, and owe a lot of money they've borrowed from me and others? Am I supposed to forget that one of my managers, and a friend, sunk so far in lonely depression during this lockdown that he took his own life? Or when I look at my financial books and realize how much I've lost over the past two months, or really the past year, and the extent of loss that restaurants like mine have suffered, can I be happy? Or that I live in a town that although showed compassion and listened to our constant pleas for help, always claimed their hands were tied and did nothing? Or once again be the target of hateful criticism on social media from those who still believe the best way to handle the virus spread is for everyone to just stay home? There is little joy left.

But sometimes things happen in life that put us directly on the path of greater things.

The challenge of serving dinner to guests at makeshift tables set in an outdoor area intended for parking cars is nerve-racking as wind gusts and rogue rain-clouds push over the mountains and surprise us at the worst times. Every day, I have to schedule additional service staff to manage this area who end up working twice as hard and making half as much as normal. Just getting a customer another glass of wine from a far-away bartender takes an eternity in table-service time and keeping track of who is where makes the front desk hosts frustrated and short tempered as they try to convince guests to have dinner on cold, broken asphalt. In a business that's focused on making people happy, it's an embarrassing situation, but for now, there's no choice. All the while, our beautiful dining room sits quiet and useless. Months pass, and each week, we comb the internet in hopes that the governor and his advisors retract the crippling mandate. But nothing. Most unfair is the fact that many other areas, some just a short drive away, are open for inside service. Little makes sense.

One day, I begin to hear rumors that inside dining will soon be allowed. Sure enough, in a sick irony, the opening date is announced—exactly one year to the day from the original shutdown date, that infamous St. Patrick's Day when it all started. Excited as we are to open our dining rooms, restauranteurs still must contend with a fearful public who reluctantly sits inside, as though we're suggesting they dine in a contaminated, biohazardous area. Some people don't care where they sit, others refuse and just leave. The challenges continue. But I suppose, as the phones ring and our guests and friends walk through our front door, thrilled to be back, to sip a martini and have dinner with us, we will all, under our masks, begin to smile again.

Slowly over the following months, as vaccinations come, I sense a change. Customers proudly announce their vaccinations as they arrive at the restaurant and would celebrate the event at the bar. An ease was taking the place that fear controlled for so long. Then, one joyous day, the long-awaited announcement comes—no more masks, and we are left with one final reason to celebrate. Those horrible, suffocating, restraining straps of fibers and fabric that we all had to wear for more than a year, through long shifts, 100-degree temperatures, that irritated our faces, and were often the cause of harsh criticism from customers who felt they weren't being worn correctly, were now unnecessary. It was time to put what happened behind us. The war was finally over.

Looking back over the year, throughout those initial, ten weeks in lockdown and all the months I spent really doing nothing, anxiously waiting for things to go back as they were, I always felt as though I should be working. It was unsettling to just sit around. At home, as I lie in bed, I think about why this all happened and wonder if it was perhaps nature rebalancing our great human ecosystem. Maybe it was her way of smacking us in the face. I ponder my life working night after night, and I realize I cannot remember ever making a reservation to go out for dinner on a Saturday night—instead, I have always been immersed in the throes of restaurant chaos. Despite this reality, I lie there, content, since I have learned and accept that work for me has not just been about making money—it has been what has satisfied me. It is not necessarily about what we get, but instead, about what we give.

I'm sure someday I'll call for a Saturday night reservation.

DESTINY

*"You have brains in your head. You have feet in your shoes.
You can steer yourself any direction you choose."*

DR. SEUSS

It always seemed to me that those who work quiet jobs with little public interaction, behind a desk or staring into a monitor, are much better served by exhilarating vacations of sightseeing, crowds of people, and hustling about the city. But for those of us whose lives are thrashed around by restaurant work, living with a daily barrage of issues and complications and relentless social interaction, a white sand beach, sloshing waves, and a bottle of Corona is all you need.

When retirement comes along, those who have voluntarily opted out of work in favor of social security are always the first to show up at the bar every afternoon. At three o'clock sharp, they sit on their favorite stool, and as they throw back martini number one, they lament to the bartenders how they longed to do something with their time now that they've retired. They want a purpose again—they want to *unretire*. They ask me if I could use an employee—"I'll do anything," I'd hear. They just want a reason to be somewhere and maybe to make a little pocket cash. I look at them and think, *Oh my God, I wish I had no responsibility*. I just want to lie in a lounge chair by the pool, with a mimosa in my hand, and stare at the clouds. Forever.

Dad used to say that anyone who owns a restaurant just wants to retire.

But reality is such that when many of us arrive at retirement, we are at the top of our games. We've gotten really good at what we do. A great blessing in life is the wisdom that comes to us as we get older. Many things finally make sense as we look at others and ourselves in an empathetic way. We rely on experience and years of accumulated knowledge to make decisions instead of reacting with rash emotion. Our priorities fall to order, developing a better financial understanding, and although more cautious about taking risks, fear isn't ruling our choices. Teenagers work to have money for the weekend, but as we age, we save for retirement. We develop patience and unquestionably tend to put up with more shit than before. Somehow, intuitively, we have learned to recognize the solutions to other people's problems, as we are divinely bestowed with long-awaited clarity, understanding, and peace.

And then we're supposed to retire? After a life of climbing a mountain, how long do we really want to just sit and enjoy the view at the top? Is retirement based on broken assumptions that this is what we want—to do nothing?

Many studies have shown that there are certain traits that those who live to be one hundred have in common. Of all the factors—good diet, exercise, reading, visiting the doctor—way on top of the list is the importance of having a purpose. You must be important to other people and have value; you must wake up each morning with a plan for the day, something that needs to be done, and be socially engaged. Freud said the most essential things in life are to have love and meaningful work. In Okinawa, Japan, a town with one of the highest percentages of old people in the world and the lowest death rate from common diseases, the elders live with their children and many make it to be well over one hundred. Some of this is due to diet—lots of fish, soy, and legumes, low saturated fat, and little to no sugar, but the grandfathers of the families still have responsibility—they fish. They wake up with the sun and, with a pail and a rod in their hand, slowly walk to the sea, where they spend the mornings alongside their friends, trying to catch dinner. The grandmothers are home, meticulously maintaining the gardens—it is work that must be done. As you walk through the town, you see them alongside the houses, kneeling in the dirt, tying cucumber vines to wired trellises to save space. There's a Japanese word for this belief, *ikigai*, which roughly translates to "the reason you wake up in the morning." It's the thing that drives you most, that gets you out of bed, and that keeps you from sinking into depression or boredom.

One of the most beautiful sights I've ever witnessed was in the remote town of Xi'an, China. Surrounded by the hustle of a modern city was a small, central park built inside a forest of bamboo clusters. The tree stalks were tall and dense, and the breeze made a whistling sound as it rustled through the top leaves. It was tranquil and calm, providing a natural shelter from the hurried traffic just outside. A maze of white limestone pathways was cut around the trees where elderly Chinese would stroll and chat during the day. As I walked, I could hear faint singing in the distance. When I made it to the central area, I noticed a pavilion, or maybe a temple, and a gathering of dozens of people, shoulder to shoulder, some holding hands, all singing what I later learned to be old Chinese hymns. They were all in their senior years, seemingly healthy, standing tall and straight without walkers or even canes, and proudly sung with loud, shrill voices. I was told this was a daily event, and all would attend.

Off to the side of the large, open plaza, I noticed a man standing alone. He was very old, with short-clipped white hair, a long, white goatee, and he stood a little crooked. As I got closer, I could see him holding a stick, like a broom handle, on the end of which he had fastened a sponge cut to a point-shape. Near his feet was an old tin can half full of black-tinted water. This was his ink. He dipped the sponge in the can and was drawing large, Chinese calligraphy on the white limestone pavement, each character about a foot square, perfectly scribed, and it covered most of the plaza. Every morning, he came to paint a poem, something he wrote specifically for the day, that would linger until it was washed away the next day by the park cleaners or by the evening rain. I asked a local how long he had been doing this. She told me as long as she could remember. "He is a poet," she said. "It is what he does."

How you are when you are young is how you will be when you are old. Our essence does not change.

When I was a boy, my mother tells me I never stopped; there was always something to do. I walked fast then, and I walk fast now. My friends and I were constantly busy. We built a different treehouse every summer, or if we were lucky, someone in the neighborhood bought a new refrigerator and the giant box it came in became our private retreat, at least until the rain took it down. In the winter, we worked for a week laying out a course for our sleds, clearing brush and packing the snow just right to prevent us from flying off the sides. We always had some sort of project going on that we had to finish so we could begin something else.

As I got older, I became fascinated with a cool, metal globe that Dad bought me one birthday. Each country was a different color, and I could name them all. In college, I worked as much as possible and every summer bought a plane ticket to some destination where I would walk the streets, eat the food, and talk with the people. At twenty-eight, I had three jobs, one of which turned into my first restaurant, and since then, it has just kept going. I still cannot sit quietly. Even this book is testament to my restlessness. There is always something going on, something to do, or to build, or to make happen—it is the way I am—it is the way my dad taught me. He was the same. It is in the core of my nature, my destiny, and just as it is for everyone, God has a way of pushing us along to get to where we're supposed to be.

Retirement? Sure, someday, but when it comes around, I can assure you I will not be sitting on a barstool sipping a martini at three in the afternoon. Well, maybe if I'm waiting for a flight—I know there are still so many wonders on that old globe for me to discover. And you can be damn sure I will do my best to hold on to my *ikigai*—to have that purpose, that reason for being, that feeling of fulfillment and accomplishment every single day, and to remain young at heart.

For more than a half century I have been running through those swinging doors. I have met a million people and have learned so much. As I sit here a happy man looking back at it all, I know deep inside that the universe has blessed me, and I am humbly grateful for the golden ticket that I was given. Yes, there has been a fair share of luck along the way, but I surely believe that the energy you put out in the world someday comes back to meet you. It has been quite the journey, and just maybe, in one small sense, my story will guide someone else along their bumpy way.

One thing I learned for sure—if you love what you do, you will be successful.

Many years ago, I had a reading by a Vedic astrologer. As he sat and studied my chart, at one moment, he looked up at me, paused, and said with his Indian accent, "You will live two lifetimes in one."

I said nothing.

He then said, "And, you are a teacher."

I responded, "No, I am not a teacher."

He said, "Well, you must be. It is here."

Will there be another restaurant? My brain tells me hell no, but I have never really listened to my brain. That great, raucous energy that lives in the souls of all restaurateurs always seems to wake up my sleeping monster. We always keep coming back for more.

And so, it goes.

ACKNOWLEDGMENTS

"None of us is as smart as all of us."

KEN BLANCHARD

My first draft of this book was just me telling the story to myself. Moving forward from that early computer file of jumbled memories to actually seeing a printed book, holding it in my hand, and giving it to someone was a process that came together through the work of a band of pros whom I'd like to applaud—James O. Fraioli, culinary book publisher and literary connoisseur, without whose guidance I might still have this book buried somewhere on a flash drive, I thank you once again for directing my path. English scholar and copy editor Nicole Frail, who touched my prose with her magic wand and fixed the thousands of tiny comma edits and grammatical screw-ups laced throughout this manuscript, I thank you for your meticulous work. And Alan, Ian, and Roger for their collective energy in producing such a beautifully wrapped package of interior layout and printing.

The production of the book's cover was a collaboration of artists—Scott McGillivray, talented graphic designer who patiently listened to my unremitting comments, and photographers Jeff Tucker and Kevin Hossler, the phenomenal photographic team who masterfully captured the essence of the book using light, color, and image composition. For me, there is no greater joy in life than working with professionals who know what they're doing—you could not have made me happier. My thanks to you all so very much.

When Suzanne Somers first stepped through my restaurant door in her pink angora sweater, tight, little skirt, and matching spiked heels, she had the aura of a star glowing around her. From my days in Hollywood restaurants, I saw it many times—it's just something special, that *je ne sais quoi* of shining energy some people possess that attracts others. Suzanne most certainly has it. Behind her radiance is a beautifully kind woman, caring, affable, and ever so bright. She is a brilliant writer who pays attention to the world, and she and I share a delicious food-bond. Thank you, Suzanne, for your thoughtful words and friendship.

And then, so importantly, my humble gratitude goes to that mighty population of restaurant disciples who diligently work on both sides of the kitchen doors and for whom this story is a daily reality. You are what gets me out of bed in the morning. I am just one link in a great chain, and it's because of all these remarkable people, and many others, that I was able to write this book.